For Carol

MORE PAPERS
FROM THE POTTING SHED

Charles Elliott

FRANCES LINCOLN LIMITED
PUBLISHERS

Frances Lincoln Limited
4 Torriano Mews
Torriano Avenue
London NW5 2RZ
www.franceslincoln.com

First Frances Lincoln edition: 2006

British Library Cataloguing in Publication data
A catalogue record for this book is available from the British Library.

ISBN 10: 0-7112-2633-4
ISBN 13: 978-0-7112-2633-3

Printed and bound in Singapore
by KHL Printing Co Pte Ltd

2 4 6 8 9 7 5 3 1

Contents

Introduction

I'm a believer in introductions. I obediently read them before reading the attached book, on the principle that you may thereby get a hint about whether there is any point in proceeding. Thus a satisfactory introduction should make clear the drift of the book, and explain why we are here. If the present paragraphs strike you as somewhat lacking in this regard, I can only apologize. I'm dealing with a tough subject, or rather wandering about in an extremely spacious field.

Nominally, this is a book about gardening. You could call it a miscellany, or a gallimaufry, or a potpourri, or something even less complimentary, and I wouldn't object. Gardening, I have found, is one of those subjects that shades off into dozens of others — history, science, biography, cultural criticism, personal experience — and so far as I'm concerned, there's no reason not to go wherever your curiosity takes you. So you will find here essays on what might be regarded as a fairly preposterous range of topics, from medieval grafting practices to excuses for banning leaf blowers, from my own adventures with birds to the history of guano. What you won't find, I guarantee, is useful information about designing a city garden or propagating auriculas. Plenty of other books can help you there. With pictures, too.

Many of these pieces have been published previously in American or British magazines, sometimes in other forms, and I am grateful to the various editors for their broadmindedness. I continue to be grateful to London's splendid libaries – the British Library, the Royal Horticulural Society's Lindley Library and, above all, the London Library, one of the world's most pleasant places.

In Offence of Birds

Like most gardeners, I am of mixed minds about birds. I can —
and do — appreciate the fact that they are ornamental, and
someone more scientifically competent than I could probably
prove that, like bees, they serve a useful purpose in the Great
Chain of Being. Assuming they do, I can put up with their
tendency to strip the cherry tree of cherries, the blueberry bushes
of blueberries, the raspberry canes of raspberries, and so on.
That's annoying but there is after all such a thing as netting. My
problem with birds is different. It's that they make a godawful lot
of noise, mostly at inconvenient times of the day, or rather night.

I once had a house in the Berkshire Hills of Western
Massachusetts that was amply furnished with birds. Phoebes
nested in the porch rafters, robins (American version) stalked the
lawn looking for worms, crows brayed in the meadow and on
autumn evenings geese honked low across the valley on their way
south. Peaceful indeed. But on the morning of May 5, 1984, at
precisely 5:22 (the time is imprinted on my memory), peace ended.
I was sleeping soundly when there was a sudden noise, a heart-
stopping noise. It sounded like a cluster of firecrackers going off
a few yards from my ear, but with a distinctive metallic *clang*. I
recognized that clang: it came from the gutter just above the open
bedroom window. Once I collected my shattered senses I knew

what made it — a woodpecker labouring under the impression that he had found the hollowest tree in the whole world.

Lying there wondering how long it would take him to recognize his error, I dimly remembered something. For several summers, a woodpecker had put in a fair amount of time battering on a telephone switch box attached to a pole across the road. We thought it was funny and made weak jokes about it ('Once he gets in there, whose party line do you think he'll eat first?'). Though you could hear him well enough (he sounded like somebody firing short M-16 bursts into a large tin can) he was too far away to bother us. *This* was different.

5:31am. Another barrage from the gutter, slightly more frenzied. I got up, went to the window, removed the screen with some difficulty and leaned out. The bird zoomed off, chattering. Ten minutes later he was back.

At this point I went out to the barn, got a long stick, and returned to bed, thinking dazedly that if he could beat on the gutter, I could, too. Next time he did, I did. He flew off. And came back.

Need I continue? Each morning that weekend we celebrated the dawn together, the woodpecker and I, alternately banging on the gutter till the heavens rang. On Monday, back in my office in the city and slightly deafened, I telephoned my friend the Distinguished Bird Expert in the hope of getting an explanation of what was going on and, if possible, a solution. He advised that the bird was apparently engaging in an activity called 'drumming', which involved showing off, or establishing territorial claims, or expressing vernal high spirits (nobody's too sure, and woodpeckers aren't talking). He had two suggestions for contending with the phenomenon.

The first suggestion was to get a mattress pad and drape it over the gutter. This I quickly dismissed as impractical; it sometimes rains in the Berkshires and a gutter full of mattress pad doesn't work very well. The second suggestion was to get an owl. This struck me as having real possibilities, except that I didn't have an owl and knew no one who did. Maybe I could carve an owl, or sew one together? The lucky discovery of a plastic owl in a garden centre saved me trying. All you had to do was to blow it up like a beach ball, and Bob's your uncle! A great horned owl (*Bubo virginianus*) to the life.

Woodpeckers indeed do not like owls. My woodpecker stayed well clear of the owl, which I had attached to the end of the gutter. In fact he stayed twenty feet away, which unhappily placed him at the precisely opposite end of the gutter, which he chose to use as a base for an acoustical tour of the whole premises: a rat-tat-tat on the Curve Ahead sign across the road, a nostalgic fusillade on the telephone switch box, a thump or two on a handy dead elm, and finally a rousing BANG BANG BANG on the gutter. His persistence was terrifying. The Distinguished Bird Expert had intimated that once the woodpecker found himself a mate and settled down to a bit of domesticity, the racket might stop. But the weekends passed, and the woodpecker didn't. Mostly he worked out in the early mornings, with an occasional midday session to keep his beak blunt; I got into a regular routine of rolling out of bed to drive him off with a stick. One day in desperation I went so far as to construct a bird scarer, a sort of clapper made out of two pieces of board hinged at one end and lashed with rubber bands. I fastened it to the window sill with a C-clamp. The idea was that I could operate it without getting out of bed by pulling a string that ran from the clapper over the curtain rod to the bed. This lifted the clapper's top board, which when you let go snapped down with a very satisfying whack. Of course the string broke; so did the curtain rod. I fixed the curtain rod.

Then one morning there was blessed silence. Well, not quite absolute silence – the tree sparrow chirped, a few crows cawed. But no woodpecker! He was gone, and I never saw – or heard – him again. I expect he drifted off to raise a family of small woodpeckers capable of quarrying trap rock armed with nothing but their beaks.

I am pleased to report that the place I live these days in West London harbours no woodpeckers, at least no woodpeckers with a fixation on gutters. What we have instead are blackbirds, birds that are quite as able to murder sleep as any woodpecker, and moreover competent to do it without the assistance of metallic objects.

In our neck of the woods, the song of the resident blackbird is a sure sign of spring. It is equally a sure sign that 4am has arrived and there's no hope of any more rest.

Have you ever studied a blackbird's song? I mean studied it singlemindedly, listening to trills and crotchets as if you were a scholar analyzing a Bach chorale? This can be done to best effect at four o'clock in the morning. There is absolutely nothing to distract you, such as sleep or sunlight or pleasant thoughts. On the contrary, it is dark and a mood of hopelessness tends to concentrate the wide-awake mind. Each sound seems etched in ice. You find yourself listening for repetitions, searching in spite of yourself for patterns in the melody. And what's worse, finding them.

According to scientists who have studied blackbird singing (presumably at a more civilized hour), 'Each burst of song varies but . . . is made up from a set repertoire of phrases.' Frankly, this seems to me to diminish matters. A blackbird may not be able to rise to the grandeur of Beethoven's Ninth, but there's something absolutely magisterial about his command of the decibels, to say nothing of the way he swings fearlessly up and down the scale in the course of concocting his melody. That he chooses to do this

CHALLENGES

while sitting on top of the television antenna next door, roughly twenty feet from our bedroom window, must be laid to artistic licence rather than pure thoughtlessness.

Needless to say, there are positive aspects to this matitudinal chorusing. Wallace Stevens, in his delightfully tangential poem 'Thirteen Ways of Looking at a Blackbird', remarks, for example:

> I do not know which to prefer,
> The beauty of inflections
> Or the beauty of innuendoes,
> The blackbird whistling
> Or just after.

I suspect I'd plump for just after. Or quite a long time after, given the choice.

Exactly why blackbirds carry on the way they do remains something of a mystery, although ornithologists offer a number of explanations that uncannily resemble those given by the Distinguished Bird Expert regarding the woodpecker's behaviour. One is that they are showing off in order to attract a mate. Male birds, it seems, get a blast of hormones in the spring, which stimulate song. This figures, especially since you frequently hear another singer, presumably female, replying at a distance. Another reason may be territoriality; i.e. I was here first, don't mess with my back garden. Or it may be simply that the bird feels good and singing makes it feel even better. Curiously, one thing that *doesn't* seem to be going on, according to experts, is straightforward competition between males to see who can sing best, a kind of Meistersinger of Hammersmith contest. Blackbirds apparently have more serious matters in mind, like imitating car alarms and ringing telephones.

Now that our blackbird has moved on to singing during the daytime – the usual pattern as spring progresses into summer – I've come round to thinking that his performance has basically to do with nervous aggression. Listen to how he literally attacks the notes, one energetic crescendo after another, one glissando on the heels of the first. You can feel the anger. This is a bird with issues.

Such an analysis may reflect my own attitude to morning birdsong. Possibly, however, blackbirds have a right to be worried. Browsing the Internet I learned that you can buy a blackbird-song ringtone for your mobile. What this might lead to in terms of adding to the cacophony is bad enough, but think what it could mean to a real-life yellowbeak searching for a mate, defending his territory, or bashing out a cadenza in E double-flat for the sixteenth time that morning. You'd be worried too.

Weedlings and Seedlings

I had a great idea for a book some years ago. It would be called *Weedlings and Seedlings* and it would help the ignorant gardener tell good seedlings from unwanted weeds. This was not a whimsical notion. At the time I had just carefully pulled out and discarded an entire planting of larkspur, under the impression that it was some kind of daisy – a weed, anyway. So I figured that if the gardener had a handy way to distinguish good things from bad things (in infancy, as it were), surely that would be a valuable addition to his tactical armoury. Maybe not on a level with his Felco secateurs and the stainless-steel fork, but still useful.

The book remains unwritten. I did attempt some research on the subject, but finally concluded that it was beyond me. For somebody who finds it difficult to locate correct identities in a guide to large mammals, pinning a name to a just-emerged seedling is a lot to ask. Besides, I lived in America when the idea first arrived, and now I live in England. The weeds, I find, are not the same in both countries, although they are equally little-loved.

I spend a lot of time dealing with weeds. While the glib comment that a weed is only a plant in the wrong place may be true, it does little to comfort those of us who appreciate a degree of order. The only real answer here is to get down on one's knees with some plausible tool and set to. A long daisy prod or dandelion digger or fish-tail weeder (the names vary, but it has a forked tip at the end of a ten-inch steel stem) is one of my favourites.

It is of course detail work. You can't clear large areas with a daisy prod. For that you need a strategic approach. In a vegetable garden with parallel rows, there's much to be said for an old-fashioned hoe, provided you work systematically forwards *towards* the weeds, instead of backing up and attempting to hoe and rake up the cut weeds at the same time. (In that case, you'll end up with a big unmanageable pile of mixed earth and weeds.) A still grander method, one which I tried this year for the first time, is to spray the whole vegetable patch with glyphosate several weeks before you intend to plant it. Provided your asparagus bed is nowhere near, this is safe and effective. You may get as much as six weeks of unencumbered bliss before the weeds pull themselves together and start growing again like billy-o.

What is it with weeds, anyway? Where do they come from? Are they always just there, lurking, waiting to sprout? Don't they ever get tired?

In the first place, we must accept that weed seeds are ubiquitous. You simply can't get away from them. In *The Origin of Species* Charles Darwin describes an experiment with results that, if you contemplate their true meaning, are enough to chill the blood of any gardener. He took three tablespoonfuls of mud from under water at the edge of a pond in February and kept it covered in his study for six months. As each plant emerged, he pulled it up and kept count. In the end the total was 517 plants of many different kinds – and all from less than a cupful of earth!

Now it's possible that a few of Darwin's seedlings were potentially valuable, but I think it safe to assume that they were mostly weeds. When we consider how many cupfuls of earth – and thus how many seeds – may be found in the average herbaceous border, it hardly bears thinking about. Efforts to reduce their number, in the circumstances, are probably doomed. Yet I, like most gardeners, keep trying.

For example, there's compost. A proper compost pile, as all the books say, is meant to heat up to the point where weed seeds are killed off, or at least rendered inactive by high temperatures. My compost heap, admirable as it is in other respects, never heats up that way. It makes perfectly beautiful crumbly brown compost in a year out of hay, leaves and manure, but in the process heats up only enough to keep the weed seeds comfortably warm during the winter. Spreading the finished product, I have to assume, is like spreading some infernal mixture of dandelion fluff, grass seed, and the generative parts of dock.

I have not found a dependable answer to this problem, except to omit the hay, concentrating on leaves. (There's reason to hope that leaves harbour no weed seeds.) I have thought about leaving the manure out as well, but manure makes the whole thing go. (Leaves alone take years to break down, in my experience, possibly because I have a lot of walnut leaves which smell wonderful but resist decay.) Opinion seems to differ about which kind of manure is infested with fewer weed seeds. I'm prepared to testify that horse manure contains an extremely wide and fascinating selection.

It's no use waiting for weed seeds to get old and die. The plants may conk out but many seeds are practically immortal. A number of splendid studies have confirmed this sad fact. Henry David Thoreau, who spent years writing a book about the dispersion of seeds, maintained that certain weed seeds could live for centuries. He found several distinctive 'rank weeds' growing in the cellar of a house that had been torn down 150 years before. Researchers in the United States Department of Agriculture Seed Testing Laboratory buried seeds of 107 species and tested them for germination at various intervals up to 39 years. At the end of the time more than a third – including red clover, common mullein, bindweed, ragweed and Scotch thistle – were still raring to go. It's said that a single large plant of curly dock (*Rumex crispus*) can produce 30,000 seeds in one season, half of which are still able to germinate after fifty years. According to *Outwitting Weeds* by Peter Loewer, however, the champions for longevity have to be the seeds of arctic lupine (*Lupinus arcticus*) found frozen in a rodent burrow in the Yukon and dated to about 8,000 BC. Planted, they grew.

Moreover, weeds have other devices besides seeds for avoiding extinction. The most famously awful aggressors – I'm thinking of Japanese knotweed, various varieties of dock, bindweed and yellow oxalis – are quite able to multiply themselves using no more than fragments of root, rather as if humans were able to reproduce from fingernail clippings. This presents a mechanical challenge to the poor gardener, who must decide whether it is better to dig, thereby risking the possibility of a dozen healthy new knotweeds in place of one dead one, or simply to ignore the interloper and go off to deadhead the roses. The late great Geoff Hamilton, whose tactics for dealing with weeds did not include the use of herbicides, confessed his terror in the face of such botanical vigour. He describes nailing a big old dock root to a shed door, leaving it there exposed to sun, wind, and frost for two years, then planting it – only to see it spring into new life 'as if the rest had done it good'.

Given that we are never really going to defeat weeds, it may make sense to relax, learn their names, and find something to admire in them. I've never tried nettle soup, but I ate a dandelion by accident last week and it wasn't bad. Poppies are pretty. Fat hen (*Chenopodium album*), which shoots up all over the vegetable garden whenever your back is turned, is supposed to be a spinach substitute. Bees like groundsel and red campion. You can make a peashooter out of a stalk of Japanese knotweed. And so on. Somehow it doesn't make me feel any better.

On Growing Potatoes

There are many extremely sound reasons not to grow potatoes. I know most of them first hand, but I still grow potatoes.

To begin with, there's scab. It is, presumably, a disease; all I know about it is that it causes peculiar unattractive rough patches to develop on the skin of the tubers. You can get rid of it by peeling the potatoes, but it can be off-putting.

Then there are eelworms and slugs, creatures disposed to bore tunnels like miniature moles directly into the potato's flesh, leaving discolored galleries and sometimes entirely hollowed-out potatoes. Again, these portions can be cut away (unless the whole potato is affected) but it not unknown for the slug himself to pop out while you are doing this. This can be discouraging if not downright revolting.

Potato blight is yet another drawback. It has a tendency to come along in midsummer just as you are relaxing, having long since hilled up the rows, made sure the haulms (nice word, haulms – it's the part of the potato plant above ground) had received adequate water, cleared out the weeds and were ready to sit down. You can tell blight has arrived when brown spots appear on a leaf or two, gradually (and then rapidly) spreading to more leaves and whole plants, and finally whole rows. It's mortal.

But perhaps the best reason not to grow potatoes is the one you hear most from non-gardeners: they are ridiculously cheap and easy to buy, and no supermarket, no matter how remote or primitive, is ever without them. Indeed, what with the increasing sophistication of our retailing magnates, you can even get some fairly unusual varieties out of the bins, often already washed. I have even heard rumours of semi-cooked potatoes for those too world-weary to face twenty minutes next to a hob. So why go to the trouble of growing potatoes yourself?

Believe me, this is a question I've pondered more than once, most recently yesterday. It is now mid-August, the sun is blinding hot in a decidedly un-British way and I have just dug a whole row of Charlotte salad potatoes. The row is about 20 feet long and contains twelve or fifteen plants; each plant harbours, I find, at least ten potatoes ranging in size up to a pound each. That is a lot of potatoes. Mind you, they are lovely potatoes, provided you ignore slug damage, with virtually no scab. But what on earth will I do with two large sacks of potatoes in a family of two? Especially when two more healthy rows of second earlies await digging?

What I would have preferred was to extract the Charlottes gradually, as we needed them, a plant or two at a time. That's the way I usually harvest potatoes, and it usually works. Of course, towards the end of the summer the slug holes are always much more in evidence (by late September all the neighbourhood slugs have apparently got the word and converge on my potato patch) but you get only the potatoes you need, as you need them. This year, however, it looks rather as though late blight has struck. The haulms have been turning brown and dying down. Admittedly, there is no sign of the powdery spore deposits that are supposed to encircle each brown blotch on the leaves. But on advice from my countryside guru Hugh Fearnley-Whittingstall, I have decided to assume the worst and take action.

In South Devon, where Fearnley-Whittingstall has his place, he claims that late blight is endemic and that you need a particular strategy for dealing with it. As soon as half the plants have collapsed, he says, you should cut the whole row to the ground, hauling the tops away for burning, then wait a week (some books say three weeks) for the spores to disperse and die. Then you lift the potatoes. All the potatoes. At that stage, having let your crop dry off in the sun and eaten as many slightly defective potatoes as you possibly can, you must figure out some suitable storage method.

The traditional method is to build what's called a 'clamp' – a pile composed of potatoes, straw and earth, preferably under cover. This strikes me as an open invitation to mice and other predators, if not slugs, so in the past when faced with a glut I've tried spreading the potatoes on and under sheets of newspaper in a dark corner of the garage. This works moderately well, except that a year later I was still finding dessicated tubers in odd corners. This time I'm using a couple of burlap bags and trying to stir up some potato-enthusiasm among the neighbours.

Of course it's possible that my Charlottes didn't have late blight at all, but some other malady – or perhaps had simply matured to the point where they said 'to hell with it' (figuratively speaking) and stopped growing. Potatoes can be mysterious things. Scab has never been a big issue for me, touch wood – I'm told that you can contend with it by putting a layer of grass cuttings into the trench before depositing the seed potatoes and covering them. I've never found this necessary. In any case, over the years I've had much more trouble with slugs than with disease; sometimes, come September, I can hardly find a tuber without at least one hole bored in it.

So dealing with slugs has been a priority at Towerhill Cottage. Hugh F.-W. doesn't seem to have anything to offer on this front, but a quick tour around the Internet has yielded some helpful information. Apparently the worst culprits are keeled slugs (*Milax* species) which can feed above ground but do most of their dirty work beneath it. Theoretically, at least, the most efficient way of getting at them should be a lethal drench of some kind, but I understand from a neighbouring farmer with a couple of acres of potatoes that the chemicals required are no longer available to amateurs like me. This is probably just as well. Non-professionals *are* permitted to use pathogenic nematodes (the resoundingly named *Phasmarhabditis hermaphrodita*, available at a price from garden supply companies), a biological control which attacks slugs. And ordinary slug pellets sprinkled among the potato plants are said to do some good, in spite of the keeled slug's subterranean habits.

There are two other anti-slug tactics, neither wholly satisfactory. The first is to plant a cultivar relatively less susceptible to slug and eelworm damage; this year I have had luck with a variety called Remarka. Slugs have so far left it mostly alone, although this may be a function of the drier-than-usual summer weather or a newly sited potato patch. On the other hand, the same source that recommended Remarka also recommended Charlotte for its slug-repellent qualities, and my Charlottes are pretty well perforated. The other solution to the slug menace is to lift your whole crop as soon as it is mature, so as to deprive the marauders of access. Which brings us right back to the glut and storage problem again.

So given the frustrations involved, does it really make any sense to go on growing potatoes? With me, the question arises afresh each spring and is always answered in the same way. I love to eat potatoes, and there is nothing like a potato out of your own garden. Where can you buy a lovely little yellow oval Charlotte with skin so delicate that you merely wipe it off? Where can you find a knobbly Pink Fir Apple whose very aroma while steaming suggests melted butter? Slice a Belle de Fontenay straight from the ground, dry the slices on kitchen towel, fry them gently in goose fat and when they are browned add a sliced onion that has been separately stewed in butter – perfection indeed, and answer enough, if any were really needed, to why we (I, anyway) grow our own potatoes.

The World of Worms

We have plenty of wildlife in and around our garden, and to tell the truth I would happily do without most of it. Rabbits, slugs, bud-eating tits, moles, even deer – we've got the lot, and you are welcome to them. The sooner the better, in fact. But there is one variety of beastie that I'd hate to give up – the lowly but indispensable worm.

It might be appropriate at this point to launch into a hymn of praise to the earthworms at work in our borders and vegetable patch, busily aerating the soil, breaking down organic matter, improving the drainage and incidentally providing a tasty diet for the moles. The worms certainly deserve congratulations. As Darwin once observed, 'it may be doubted whether there are many other animals which have played so important a part in the history of the world'. Personally, I can't speak for the world, and Darwin's take on the little wrigglies was far more comprehensive than mine. In the course of his research he even had one of his sons play his bassoon to a worm to see whether it could hear (it couldn't). Yet the presence of worms has made my own small part of the world a better place.

I speak now not merely of worms at large. For the past six or eight years (apart from a short hiatus I will explain in a moment) we have harboured a contingent of worms in captivity, too. They live in a plastic rubbish-bin-like container with a hinged lid situated (in the summertime) under a clump of Lawson cypresses not far from the kitchen door or (in winter) in a nearby shed. Inside the bin, in addition to the worms, is a mass of decaying vegetable matter – potato peelings, eggshells, banana skins, superannuated tomatoes, the aging edges from lettuce leaves, all manner of non-meat plate scrapings, and a number of other substances capable of dissolution under worm attack. It all smells as you might expect.

This affair is called a wormery. It may have been a gift from a thoughtful relative, but at this point I can't be sure. I still remember how simple and practical it seemed when it first arrived, along with a small brown pasteboard box full of worms and a sack of calcified seaweed. All you had to do was to insert the base, thereby raising the floor of the bin so the worms wouldn't drown in collected liquid, tear up some newspaper, dampen it, pitch in the worms and you were on your way, all ready to compost anything from a leek top to an over-the-hill Beurre d'Anjou.

And, by George, it worked! Whatever you put in there soon collapsed into what you might call its essence, or at least something taking up a great deal less space than it did to begin with. From time to time I hoisted the bin up on to a low wall and opened a tap conveniently placed near the bottom, draining off a gallon or so of translucent brown 'juice' reputed to be an excellent fertilizer when diluted ten-to-one with water. I never saw a worm, except for some minuscule infants apparently trying to escape via the loose-fitting lid; they were in any case a special breed of red worm, particularly suited to compost duty, that much preferred to hide in darkness. To anyone faced with the odorous job of feeding or draining the bin, their name will come as no surprise: *Eisenia foetida.*

For a couple of years all went well with our foetid friends. I filled numerous five-litre plastic bottles with liquid fertilizer, while Carol assiduously furnished them with a running supply of kitchen debris. They devoured it. As advised in the instructions, I occasionally sprinkled calcified seaweed over the working mass, which was supposed to reduce the acidity and cheer up the worms. Once or twice, without notable success, I attempted to dig out some of the decayed material, promptly burying it under leaves in my regular compost heap to avoid asphyxiating everyone in the neighbourhood.

Then gradually it became obvious that something was wrong. There was no sign of any worms. Not that there had been much obvious sign before but now the peelings and cabbage leaves were simply piling up in the bin, uneaten. Holding my nose, I made an exploratory sortie. Not a worm.

I suppose that we might at this point have given up, emptied the bin and concentrated on another form of fertilizer, say dead fish. But you get fond of worms. I telephoned the company in Devon responsible for the wormery and was told that we probably needed a new batch of worms. I was also told that I should have been clearing out the compost more frequently, at least every six months. Too great a concentration of worm casts (i.e. what comes out of the other end of the worm) can be lethal to *Eisenia foetida*. It had probably been lethal to ours. I ordered a fresh boxful (450 worms, £15.90) and directed that they be delivered to my office in London.

I should explain that the wormery is located at our cottage in the Welsh Marches, but during the week we live and work in London. At this particular time we were staying in a rented third-floor flat in Chelsea while builders deconstructed our London house.

The box of worms arrived sooner than expected, on Tuesday morning to be exact. We were not due to go the country until Friday. It struck me as unlikely that 450 worms crammed into a box no more that four inches each way would be able to survive for most of a week without unpacking, so I bought a bag of compost from a garden supply shop and a white nappy pail with a lid. That night I bicycled home to the flat with the pail, now filled with compost and worms, dangling from the handlebars. The bicycle lock-up area under the stairs next to the street struck me as dark, damp and cool, a much nicer place for worms than our flat, so I left the pail down there.

The next morning, going in to get my bicycle, I was stunned to discover worms everywhere. It looked like it had rained worms. Four hundred and fifty worms is a lot of worms, and most of them seemed to be roaming among the bicycles, in the area outside, and on the stairs leading up to our landlady's apartment. I had no reason to think that her sympathies would extend to *Eisenia foetida*, so I spent a frantic half-hour worm-hunting, shoving them back into the pail (they came right back out again) and into a couple of handy planters containing rhododendrons. Finally, having corralled as many as I could, I sealed the lid with some thin brown sticky tape and went off to work, thinking worm thoughts.

It's hard to say how many worms we eventually managed to place in the wormery. There were more escapees among the bicycles that week, and a few also somehow negotiated the sticky tape during the drive to the country in the car. (I don't envy them their fate.) But it must have been enough to start a new self-sustaining colony. These days there always seems to be room for another tranche of kitchen scraps, and the magic liquid continues to accumulate in the bottom of the bin at a satisfying rate. I must have drained fifteen or twenty gallons out of it by now.

My one remaining problem is how to get the finished compost out of the bin. I gather from reading up on the subject that is known as 'harvesting', but to my way of thinking this suggests a far more salubrious process than my wormery affords. The stuff is wet, slippery and stinks to high heaven. When you remove it, moreover, you must take care not to remove the worms at the same time, so you have to encourage them to migrate out of the 'harvested' part. I'm told that this may be done by dumping the entire contents of the bin on to a plastic sheet, then progressively skimming off the top layer while waiting for the worms to burrow downwards into darkness. In time, it is said, you have nothing left but worms, and can start up your wormery all over again. I have not tried this; I'm haunted by visions of red worms wriggling off at high speed in all directions. But the time is coming when I may have to. I owe them. I want them to be happy. They're part of the family.

*   *   *

Gardeners care about worms. I think it's safe to say that almost nobody else – except possibly bait fishermen – does, at least to the same extent, or in the same way. We depend on them for all manner of seriously useful activities, mostly underground, and would be quite lost without their wriggly, boneless, slimy, indispensable presence. The rest of the world seems prepared to let worms go their way unheeded.

One who did care was Charles Darwin, author of *The Formation of Vegetable Mould Through the Action of Worms, With Observations on Their Habits*, along with a few other works. This book, his last, was a best-seller; in fact, it sold more copies even than *The Origin of Species*. Darwin was mesmerized by worms. In his view worms were responsible not only for creating, over ar immense span of time, the rich soil we depend on for growing crops, but also for burying ruins and altering the very topography of the land.

Appropriately, the writer Amy Stewart has chosen to quote at length from Darwin in *The Earth Moved*, her own updated paean to our subterranean friends.* She describes the great man cutting up bits of paper into triangles to see which corner a worm would pull into its hole; playing a piano and whistling to see whether they would respond; trying to figure out the number of worms per acre; measuring how fast they caused stones to sink into the ground; watching them by the hour in his study. He must have had a wonderful time.

Yet for all his assiduity, it is now clear that even Darwin failed to do more than scratch the surface of the earthworm world. He concentrated almost entirely on *Lumbricus terrestris*, or nightcrawlers, the big fellows that burrow deep into the earth and come out at night to forage, leaving little piles of castings on velvety English lawns. As Stewart points out, he never mentions the 'red wigglers' or epigeic worms that live near the soil surface and are now the focus of most interest and research. Then there are endogeic worms, many of which inhabit the area around plant roots and are rarely seen in public except by accident, say when a gardener is pulling a weed or transplanting a shrub.

Though not herself an oligochaetologist, Ms Stewart has dug out a lot of fascinating information about worms.

One of the most curious is their role in proving the theory of continental drift. Darwin, like other scientists of his time, was exercised by the appearance of similar species in widely separated parts of the world. After puzzling over the problem for years, he

---

* *The Earth Moved: On the Remarkable Achievements of Earthworms* by Amy Stewart (London 2004).

finally concluded that plants and animals must have drifted or been blown across the oceans. But worms don't float, live worms anyway.

It was not until thirty years after Darwin's death that what is now accepted as the real answer was proposed. The land masses themselves broke apart and drifted to far corners of the globe, carrying different species with them. Oddly, it now appears that it may be possible to figure out just how this happened by studying the distribution of worm species – why, for example, Caribbean worms are closely related to those in Fiji. Worms, after all, go way back: they survived the Great Permian Mass Extinction 248 million years ago, and another cataclysm 65 million years ago, when dinosaurs and three-quarters of all other species perished. And they don't move around much.

Worms' natural tendency to accomplish large amounts of useful work in the course of eating and defecating is of course their main appeal. *The Earth Moved* tells how they have been employed to encourage favourable bacteria and to contend with bad ones, to turn smelly sewage residues into fragrant plant food, to transform poor farm land into rich loam. (In worm-poor New Zealand, we hear, the experimental introduction of European earthworms led to a 70 per cent increase in productivity.) Worms can function like miners' canaries to detect pollution and toxins such as PCBs. They may be able to consume greenhouse gases. You have to admire the little creatures.

Ms Stewart certainly does. In addition all the hard news about worms (and a bit more propaganda for organic gardening than I find necessary) she gives us some excellent information and advice about wormeries, which in my case ought to be welcome. I wish I could say that her experience accords with mine.

She describes an orderly sort of bin populated with well-behaved, even loveable little workers producing 'a few pounds of black, rich castings' every three months or so. I rarely see a worm; she finds hers 'interesting to watch'. There isn't a word about the smell. Admittedly, her wormery sounds much better organized than mine, with separate trays that can be lifted out as they fill with those beautiful castings. Perhaps I should start all over again.

In the meantime, I was especially pleased to discover in this book the answer to a worm question I've always wondered about: if you cut a worm in two, do you get two worms? The answer is, probably not, although many species readily grow a new tail if it's cut off. *Eisenia foetida* is talented that way. It may even grow two heads.

Stretch Gardening

For roughly forty years, I have been living in a city and travelling on weekends to the country. I enjoy gardening, but gardening being a rural (or at least suburban) occupation, my gardens have always been country gardens. The trouble is that I'm a city person for four or five days a week, totally out of reach of spading fork and slug pellets. I have gradually reconciled myself to this state of affairs, to the point where I have stopped worrying about whether or not that newly planted apricot needs water today (rather than three days hence) or if my failure to find time to prune the wisteria in February will result in no blossoms. You can only assist nature, not dominate it, the more so when 148 miles of M4 lie between you and your duties.

It has taken me quite a long time to grasp this sluggard truth. As a 'stretch gardener' – one end of my garden is, so to speak, roughly two and a half hours from the other end – certain constraints are bound to be operative. You can waste an awful lot of energy trying to bridge the gap.

Nowadays I journey between Shepherds Bush and Monmouthshire with a degree of insouciance. I know I can't have a greenhouse – who would regulate the temperature, or adjust the humidity, when there's nobody around for a week at time? Even a cold frame can be chancy. All such useful devices require a human presence, and present is exactly what the stretch gardener is not.

My attitude was innocently different when I commuted weekly between New York City, where I lived and worked for many years, and an old house in the Berkshire Hills of Massachusetts. As a beginning, improbably enthusiastic gardener, I was determined to prove that there was nothing really complicated about the art, even for a part-timer. Why, for example, stock up on seedlings from a nursery, at considerable expense, if you can grow them from scratch? The books made it sound easy.

I started with geraniums. I was told that you could take a cutting, dip the cut end in rooting powder, stick it in a glass of water on a sunny windowsill. Then you could go back to the city for week, or even two, and when you returned the geranium cutting would be furry with roots and ready for planting. All true. I planted the little cutting in a pot, watered it, and drove off to New York with a feeling of accomplishment. The next weekend I found the poor thing prostrate and gasping in its bone-dry pot. While that didn't quite kill it, nothing could save it a week later when I put it outside to be nourished by the spring rains and it got snowed on.

But that sunny windowsill still seemed promising. My next move was to buy a sort of covered yellow plastic tray designed to hold eighteen round peat pots. You planted seeds in the pots, poured water into the bottom of the tray, and trusted to natural processes (which? Osmosis? Perfusion? Hydrotaxis?) to get the potting compost moist. It worked. It worked all too well. The pots were so wet that they turned green round the edges and the only seeds that sprouted promptly died of over-watering. The one exception was a pale whitish object that looked suspiciously like an Indian pipe (*Monoflora uniflora*) or some especially gloomy mushroom. On the whole, this was disappointing. The tray also smelled bad.

At this low point, just about the time I was ready to admit that absentee propagation was a bust, my brother-in-law presented me with the solution: a huge plant stand with fluorescent lights and three four-foot-long trays capable of holding some 300 seedlings. Until then it had never occurred to me to start plants *in the city* – no sunny windowsills. But now light was no problem and I wouldn't have to abandon my charges for a week at a time. I could get serious. Nothing was beyond me now.

Of course that plant stand was *big*. Unpacked, unfolded, bolted together and plugged in, it occupied roughly one third of the sitting room. The unsuitability of this arrangement was intimated to me by my wife. So I took the thing apart and moved it to my midtown office, on the 29th floor of a building on East 50th Street where I worked as an editor in a publishing house. After a certain amount of pushing and pulling it fetched up in a dark corner of the corridor next to the ladies' room in company with a plastic Christmas tree, a couple of fire extinguishers and a large pile of what publishers call 'dead matter' – nothing to do with my gardening, I hasten to say, but proofs and other debris left over after a book has been published.

My first challenge was to get the lights to work properly. The idea is that they should automatically turn on at 'dawn' and go off at 'dusk,' simulating normal outdoor light. A timer plugged into a wall socket in a nearby office and some wire pinned to the carpet with bent paperclips accomplished this nicely (and not too dangerously, American voltage being thankfully half that of British), at least until one night some miscreant stole the timer and the wire and the whole blasted thing had to be replaced.

Planting proved to be much more straightforward. Messy, though. After the fact, I have to admit that you should never attempt to soak large quantities of potting mix indoors, while squatting on the floor, no matter how many newspapers you spread out beforehand. But it was pleasant to spend one's lunch hour sowing flats and pricking out seedlings, just like a real gardener. There were times when an appointment turned up early, which could be embarrassing, but nobody complained about the sand, vermiculite and peat pots, even those colleagues required to squeeze past them on the way to the ladies' room.

Germination was terrifyingly fast. That may have had something to do with the modest amount of air available. Like most New York skyscrapers, our building was pretty well sealed off from the coarse unhealthy oxygen blowing through the canyons of Manhattan, getting its presumably purified air through an expensive series of ducts and fans instead. This system operated only when people were actually at work, from 8:00am to 5:30pm. The rest of the time whatever gas happened to be on hand simply stagnated, sullenly turning to carbon dioxide. But nothing makes a plant happier than carbon dioxide, or so I recalled from high school biology.

Still, you couldn't say that everything was coming up roses. The tomatoes got very leggy – tall, floppy, vaguely diffident, ready to be planted outdoors about four weeks before the last frost. There was a plague of aphids, which I sprayed 'according to the instructions on the label'; these may have been correct because the stuff annihilated the aphids, but the plants looked suicidal too. A cleaning lady unplugged the lights; a gin-and-tonic at an office party laid waste to an entire flat of snapdragons. Then there were the odd plants that turned up from heaven knows where, placed there for company, I suppose, or in the belief that I was running some sort of charity clinic for potted invalids. Transplanting seedlings from flats into pots took too much time to be finished during working hours and the alternative – Sunday afternoons – was when the office air supply fell to near-asphixiation levels. Getting down on the floor helped some but after a couple of hours it was difficult to get up again. More than once I expected to be found there on Monday morning, along with the other dead matter.

The trickiest part was watering. As anybody who has ever started plants from seed knows, it is depressingly easy to water too much or too little, and hard to figure out how to avoid it. The problem was magnified in an arrangement like mine. You might proceed with scrupulous care during the week, but on a fine spring weekend you probably want to go to the country. That meant at least two waterless days, more on a holiday weekend. I began by trying to soak everything thoroughly ahead of time, which worked out badly; those seedlings that hadn't died of thirst drowned or damped off by Monday. The answer was to drape big plastic rubbish bags over the light fixtures, creating curtains that reduced evaporation. All fine – except that *some* air needed to circulate. Otherwise you got a general encrustation of white mould and another bad smell, which I proved by mistakenly tucking the bags in around the bottom before one long weekend.

So I got my plants – six or eight kinds of annuals, a couple of experimental perennials (delphiniums, rudbeckia), and a slew of vegetable from leeks to plum tomatoes.

The next stage proved to be unexpectedly challenging, the essence, one might say, of stretch gardening. I had to transfer the plants from East 50th Street to my apartment in Greenwich Village to be hardened off on the fire escape before I could take them (along with two children, two cats, wife and assorted other impedimenta) by car to the Berkshires. Taxicabs and parking tickets being seriously expensive, I learned that it is possible, with care and an aggressive stance toward other rush-hour passengers likely to step on them, to take seedlings in shopping bags on the subway. Rain could be a hazard. There is nothing more depressing to the soul of a stretch gardener than the sight of a large brown paper Bloomingdale's shopping bag in a downpour melting over a precious flat of Chinese forget-me-nots.

Despite my successes, I must admit that my enthusiasm for long-distance plant propagation gradually waned while I lived in New York. When I moved to London about twenty years ago, I willed the plant stand to a fellow office gardener (who promptly moved it to Vermont, probably a wise step), and though I've tried raising plants from seed on occasion since, I've decided that the operation really belongs in the country rather than a window sill in West Kensington. These days in the country I'm experimenting with an electrically heated mat to encourage germination, and felt wicks to keep the seed trays moist while I'm in the city during the week. I have also constructed a cold frame, which may or may not offer scope for new departures. It has already been the scene of botanical carnage during our absence on holiday in Italy last year; the gadget that was supposed to open it on hot days didn't.

But it seems unlikely that I will give up being a stretch gardener, in spite of the drawbacks. It may indeed be quixotic, sowing seeds doomed to die of dehydration, pruning shrubs whose bloom we will miss, frantically weeding and mowing and raking so that everything is in perfect order for the delectation of the permanent residents – the moles. Yet compensations exist, some obvious, some less so. There is the inexplicable gratitude of city friends for surplus vegetables (even courgettes!) and herbs (basil is greeted like myrrh and frankincense). There is the preciousness of time, to a stretch gardener who has less of it; boredom is never a problem. And there is the challenge, if not to raise Himalayan gentians then at least to grow some decent asparagus. Like every other sort of gardener, in fact.

The Big Lockup

The other day – Saturday, to be exact – I decided to count the number of keys we had kicking around our house in the country. (Real keys, I mean, not the mysteriously obsolete ones that can't be identified and just accumulate because they seem too important to throw away, but aren't.) What I discovered shook me. Including such standard items as car keys and the tiny frequently lost key that you need to start the engine on the big mower, the total is something like twenty-four. The house, barn, shed and gates alone account for sixteen.

Now this is in the depths of rural Wales. I'm not talking about London (we won't even begin to think about the number of keys required there) but a pleasant countryside with a great many more sheep than people and a tradition of local amiability. It's the kind of place, you might think, where the old practice of permanently unlocked doors was invented, or where leaving the porch light on was about the biggest concession to 'security' anybody could think of. I'm depressed to report that this is no longer true. Like nearly every place else in what is pleased to call itself the civilized world, our corner of the backwoods is busy setting up fortifications. At least we are, painfully conscious of the fact that from Monday morning until Friday afternoon, we're not there.

I'm of mixed minds about this development. As far as I can recall, I never even had a house key when I was a kid at school in

Ypsilanti, Michigan, and I lived for thirty years in the heart of Manhattan without being burgled or mugged. Nobody ever stole anything from us in the Berkshires, either. On the other hand, during the last three years in Skenfrith we've been burgled successfully twice (and probably would have been a third time if the dandelion spike being used to wrench open a door hadn't broken off). It seems as though the barbarians really are at the gates – or near enough that some serious protective measures have had to be instituted.

After the first burglary – which involved the loss of such flea-marketable items as a chainsaw, a large string trimmer, a rotary saw and a power drill – I took several steps. First, I had a strong door put on a windowless stone shed, and stored the replacement tools there. Then I upgraded the locks on the barn doors and installed sensor-equipped fixtures to flood the parking area outside with light whenever anyone drove up. (Wind in a beech tree, squirrels, cats, rabbits and assorted ghosts also turn on the lights. The brochure neglected to say so, but no problem.) As the house itself had been spared – no tools there, and located far enough from the drive to deter (I figured) the average thief – my assault-proofing concentrated on the barn.

Unfortunately, the burglars also concentrated on the barn, mounting another successful raid only a few weeks ago. This time they went through one of my new locks like butter, opened the big doors and abstracted two oversize pieces of garden equipment – a heavy-duty lawnmower and an American-made rototiller weighing somewhat better than 300 pounds. I have to admire their enterprise. Simply hoisting that tiller into a van must have herniated any normal Cardiff crack addict, to say nothing of the challenge of selling it. A dusty victory, I would have thought, but from my point of view an especially annoying one. The mower was a particular favourite.

It was at this point that we really got paranoid and the keys began to multiply. A neighbour suggested building gates so that nobody could drive up the barn; we had them built (and not cheaply). New and more substantial locks went on the barn doors. Screws were replaced with stove bolts so that the hinges couldn't be removed. All the remaining mowers and garden machinery were padlocked to a steel support post with 35 feet of heavy chain. I installed window locks on every reachable window in the house. And we decided to cap it all with a burglar alarm system.

I know a lot more now about alarm systems than I did before, and I don't like much of what I know. Their dependability is questionable, they have great potential for alienating (if not worse) hitherto friendly neighbours and the police seem to regard them with a mixture of enthusiasm and utter doubt. Alarm salesmen, however, are terrific. After hearing the spiel of three different salesmen touting three different systems, I was in each case ready to sign on the dotted line. They were that convincing. In the end, however, mildly dazed by the vistas of absolute protection offered, we went with a company I shall call Renegade Security Systems Ltd.

I won't go into Renegade's scheme in detail, but as I get it the sensors they've installed are supposed to need more than simple movement to go off. The idea is to prevent false alarms from spiders and moths. (There appears to be a serious question about cats, so to play safe we keep the cats out when the system is armed.) If the alarm does go off during the week when we are away, the Renegade station down in Cardiff registers it, and calls both the police and one of our long-suffering neighbours, three of whom have been designated 'key-holders'. In theory the forces of law and order then converge on Towerhill Cottage, capturing the intruders and preventing the loss of yet another lawnmower.

I hasten to say that this has not yet happened in the weeks since we've been wired up. In fact, the worst thing that occurred took place during the installation, when a Renegade workman neatly drilled into a hidden heating pipe and flooded the place.

There have, of course, been a few glitches. The first two nights that the sensors in the barn were turned on, something or other tripped the alarm. I have a strong suspicion that the culprits were bats. The alarm, however, made such a racket that there is also reason to believe that the bats were permanently scared away. For this relief, much thanks. In any case, the police weren't called because we were still in the trial period, and for that too, I'm grateful. It has become increasingly clear to me that if you have an alarm system, you had damned well better keep on the right side of the police. Which means no false alarms.

The false alarm problem is hardly British; it's one that has been troubling police in America for years and is getting worse there. Until recently the official policy in Britain had been a limit of seven false alarms before police give up paying attention, but beginning this year you'll be allowed only five. This puts a large premium on bats. Still, I suspect that the technology has advanced somewhat since 1882, when Mark Twain wrote a short story called 'The McWilliamses and the Burglar Alarm', and noted that 'a burglar alarm combines in its person all that is objectionable about a fire, a riot, and a harem, and at the same time none of the compensating advantages, of one sort or another, that customarily belong with that combination'.

But I'm not inclined to be negative, at least not yet. By anyone's standards, I should think, Towerhill Cottage is now secure. All those keys! All that technology! All those bills! I'm impressed, so much so that I rather hoped that our insurance company might be impressed too. But the premiums have gone up again. Is Norwich Union trying to tell me something, or was that just a bat?

Asparagus

I'm beginning to think that I have finally got a grip on asparagus. This may be a foolhardy statement; I've been wrong about such things before. But last weekend we (two of us) had two substantial meals of the delicious stuff, and were able to cut enough to bring back to the city for a third meal. And that doesn't even count what's settling down in the new asparagus crib I've built.

In fact, I have every expectation that when asparagus time comes around again next spring, we will be flooded with it. A consummation devoutly, etc.

My vegetable gardening philosophy is a pretty simple and straightforward one – I grow what I like to eat, what is better fresh out of the garden, and what costs too much or is hard to find. Thus I ignore carrots, cabbages, sprouts, turnips and a lot of other things. Special potatoes (Pink Fir Apple, say, or Belle de Fontenay), French beans, lettuces, rocket, basil – all these find a place. Shallots are there, more out of habit than necessity, because they used to be hard to find in America, where I started gardening. But the prize vegetable of all, in my book, is asparagus. Anyone who has experienced asparagus minutes out of the garden, dripping with melted butter and gently touched by a few flakes of sea salt, will not need to be told why.

People seem to be put off by the fact that you can't plant asparagus and harvest it the same year. That's true – you should wait a year or two (see below) – but how many other crops can you plant once and harvest for twenty years running? On the other hand, it is possible to make mistakes with asparagus, and in the course of my horticultural adventures I've made most of them.

One mistake was to think that planting asparagus in the Welsh Marches was the same as planting it in Western Massachusetts, where winter temperatures can drop to well below –0°F (–18°C) for days at a time. In Massachusetts you worry about frost and plant deep – 4 or 5 inches isn't too much. I did the same in Monmouthshire, only to find that it was rain I should have worried about. My trench filled with water and the roots drowned.

So I tried again, planting shallowly. What I failed to consider this time was that in its natural state my soil is heavy red clay. That is, about as far as could be imagined from the light sandy loam asparagus likes, the kind of soil that made Battersea the asparagus capital of Britain for a few centuries. The first year a few extremely spindly shoots managed to force their way through the rock-hard crust. I was so delighted to see them that I promptly cut them off and ate them. Another mistake. Thereafter in spite of my attempts to ameliorate the soil – endless applications of compost, sheep manure, leaf mould, even sand – that row of asparagus always looked anorexic. It still does.

In mild frustration, if not actual despair, I planted yet another row of crowns, allowing them to grow undisturbed for two years before the first cutting, and continuing to cosset them with compost. This at last paid off. They displayed a considerably better attitude, producing spears of almost normal size, and have gone on doing so for more than ten years now. That's the asparagus we ate last weekend.

This ought to have been the happy ending of my story. As I've said, we are now getting about as much asparagus, thick and thin, as we know what to do with. But somehow the situation failed to satisfy. Two years ago, contemplating the dismal weed-studded expanse of clay that has always been my asparagus patch, it struck me that I wasn't being fair to this ambrosial vegetable. It deserved a proper home.

The result, spiked together out of a dozen logs using huge nails, is my asparagus crib. This affair is about 25 feet long, a yard wide, and a foot deep, filled with a laboriously barrowed-in mixture of sand, compost, rotted sheep manure and a little earth. Before I built it, I dug over the ground underneath, and when it was ready to plant I ordered twenty-five big, healthy two-year crowns from a grower in Norfolk. (Our local garden centre now stocks nothing but spider-sized one-year crowns in plastic.)

Apart from the fact that the cats seem to think that it is the world's biggest litter tray, the asparagus crib promises to be a success. I planted it in the autumn (shallowly) and six months later some substantial spears appeared. This spring, the second after planting, there were thirty or forty of the lovely brutes, up to three-quarters of an inch thick. I cut very few, just to be safe. Next year it ought to be ready for a full eight or ten weeks' cutting.

Only a talking asparagus plant, I suspect, could really do justice to the good points of my crib. Being dismissive may be easier (of course it is just a simple raised bed, of course the logs are bound to rot out sooner rather than later, spilling soil, asparagus and all into the nettles). But it is delightfully simple to weed — you can sit on the edge while you're doing it, and even docks come out with the slightest tug; the amount of compost and manure means that the soil retains moisture, but never becomes

Gibberellic Acid

The 1950s were a good time to be in the science department of *Life* magazine. Advertising income was up, circulation vast, weekly issues of 300 pages gave us plenty of space, and a lot of important and exciting things were going on – the development of nuclear power, the discovery of the smoking–lung cancer link, Sputnik. Something called the International Geophysical Year occupied a good deal of our time, particularly the expensive (and ultimately futile) attempt to drill the 'Mohole' through the earth's mantle. And physicists kept coming up with spectacular new subatomic theories that needed explaining. In these heady circumstances, it isn't really too surprising that the story of gibberellic acid didn't quite make it into print – in *Life* magazine, at least.

The failure was not for want of trying on the part of the press agent for the company promoting the substance as a horticultural miracle-worker. Gibberellic acid, we were told, was capable of sending plants into a positive spasm of growth and flowering. Spray a little on just about any bit of greenery and stand back – you'll be amazed! As a gesture towards substantiating these claims, the PR man gave us each a bottle of gibberellic acid and a pot of African violets, inviting us to see for ourselves.

It was a bit of a bust. I don't recall any especially spectacular results from the African violets. My potful collapsed and died when I over-watered it. Nobody else reported remarkable growth or blossoms. When it became clear that there was going to be no story, the PR man moved on to something more significant, and so did I – it was, I think, a moderately profound piece about Laika, the first dog in space. Gibberellic acid passed, so far as I was concerned, into that limbo of improbabilities already occupied by such publicity seekers as the man from Missouri who claimed his daughter could see through blindfolds. (No story there, either, although I never figured out how she did it.)

For the first time in nearly fifty years, it recently occurred to me to wonder what had become of gibberellic acid. Had it been a simple hoax? That seemed unlikely in view of the cost of hiring someone to promote it. Clearly there had been at least the prospect of commercial gain, and it sounded plausible enough. On the off chance that the Web might tell me something, I tapped 'gibberellic acid' into Google. What emerged was astounding.

In the first place, I found, the substance was legitimate enough. Gibberellic acid* is a growth-regulating hormone found in all plants, flowering and non-flowering, in algae, mosses, certain fungi and even a few bacteria. Its principal function is to make the cells in a plant's stem elongate, but it also does other more obscure things, which are only now being explored. Given the history of its discovery, it's no wonder that there has been some delay.

In Japan in the late nineteenth century farmers had noticed something odd about certain of their rice plants. Seedlings were shooting up to an unusual height, yellowing, and toppling over without producing grain. Mystified, they called the disease

---

* Technically, the term 'gibberellic acid' refers to one of a group of about ninety closely related substances called gibberellins, but it is often used to describe all of them.

bakanae – 'foolish seedling'. Scientists at first laid the problem to a *Fusarium* fungus but in 1926 botanist Eiichi Kurosawa established that the guilty party was a chemical secreted by another fungus, *Gibberella fujikuroi*. A few years later, still in Japan, the first gibberellin was isolated and named, and work began on exploring its functions. Yet in spite of the hormone's central importance to plant physiology, scientists in the West knew nothing about it. They remained ignorant for more than a decade, until World War II was over and researchers in Britain and the US finally came across the early Japanese papers.

It must have been at this point that some entrepreneur concluded that there was money in selling gibberellic acid to gardeners, and tried to get a story about it into *Life*. Not, I have to say, altogether pointlessly. It may not be magical, but trials since then have shown that it can in fact be employed to achieve an extraordinary range of useful horticultural results. These – depending on the plant and the concentration of acid applied – include overcoming dormancy and speeding germination; forcing flowering; increasing fruit set (with the resulting fruit possibly rendered partly or wholly seedless); making difficult hybridization possible; speeding up growth; and staving off frost damage. Gibberellic acid sprayed on table grapes loosens the clusters, allowing bigger grapes to form; it increases the yield of strawberries and the malting quality of barley; it makes sweet cherries firmer and bigger. In one experiment, fruit trees treated with a 1 per cent gibberellic acid paste grew 8½ feet in a year instead of the normal 1½ feet. And so on. The list of plants on which a gibberellic acid solution can be profitably employed is getting longer by the day. One assumes that the companies devoted to manufacturing the stuff (they are mostly in Mainland China) are doing pretty well too.

But there is more to the gibberellic acid story than king-sized pineapples. It is hardly too much to say that the hormone – or rather its controlled absence – has been at the heart of the greatest agricultural development of modern times, the Green Revolution, which saw the world's total grain output nearly treble in less than forty years.

As the Japanese rice farmer with his foolish seedlings learned to his cost, having plants grow tall is not necessarily a good thing. In *Oklahoma!* Curly might sing ecstatically that 'the corn is as high as an elephant's eye', but wheat farmers had long known that vigorous full-sized varieties always had a dangerous tendency to 'lodge' – be flattened by wind or rain before they could be harvested. Moreover, standard varieties wasted a lot of energy in producing long straw instead of grain. The answer – again originating in Japan – was semi-dwarf strains, particularly one called Norin, that bore more heavily and, being stocky, resisted lodging. Introduced to the US in the 1950s, further crossbred and spread widely around the world (especially to India and Mexico) along with a few dwarfed rice varieties, they served to create the Green Revolution in the 1970s.

And where does gibberellic acid come in? Just here: the wheat and rice strains were apparently dwarfed because lucky mutant genes made them unresponsive to the effects of the growth hormone. Having finally gained an understanding of gibberellic acid and the way it worked, scientists could now concentrate on techniques for blocking its action. The resulting high-yielding varieties saved millions of people from starvation.

The Green Revolution was, of course, not unadulterated good news; much has been made, and rightly, of the damage caused by some of its other aspects, such as excessive irrigation and overuse of pesticides and fertilizers. But the contribution made by research on gibberellic acid is indisputable and positive. Nor is it over yet.

In 1999, scientists at the John Innes Centre in Norwich

announced that they had managed to identify and isolate the precise single gene that makes any plant respond to gibberellic acid. They worked it out with the help of normal and dwarf forms of *Arabidopsis thaliana* (thale or mouse-ear cress), a fairly common weed. Wheat breeders had been fortunate enough to have a naturally mutant gene to play with when they created semi-dwarf varieties; until now been impossible to create dwarf versions of many other crops – some of them locally significant, like maize, millet and sorghum – in the absence of such a mutant. With the gene at hand, as the John Innes team leader Nick Harberd observed, geneticists will now be able to convert virtually any locally-adapted low-yielding variety into a potentially high-yielding dwarf form. No other characteristics of the plant need be affected, only the way it responds to the instructions of its gibberellic acid to grow tall.

Will these new varieties emerge? For the sake of feeding more millions they probably should, but the question is obviously connected to controversy about GM crops in general. Tinkering with gibberellic acid – or rather with methods of preventing it from functioning in plants – is now a matter of gene manipulation, which terrifies (illogically, in my opinion) many otherwise generous and thoughtful people.

But that's another story, a very long distance from my pot of African violets in 1957.

Blue Fruit and Chimeras

There is something alchemical about grafting, like converting lead to gold. It's easy to see why the process has always fascinated gardeners, beginning with (at least) the Greeks. Next to growing a difficult plant, what could be more challenging than to create a new one using nothing but patience, a knife, string, wax and perhaps a bit of cloth?

Conventionally, of course, grafting is used to propagate a valuable strain without changing its characteristics. That's the main point about grafting. Find a good variety of apple, graft a bud or a scion from the tree that bore it on to a suitable host stock, and you will have a new branch or tree bearing apples exactly like the old ones. The new tree may look very different, depending on the stock employed, but the fruit will be the same. It's all pretty straightforward, and a technique readily adapted to multiplying all sorts of plants from trees to shrubs to roses.

The history of grafting, however, is filled with far more eccentric enterprises. Altering the form and colour of fruit, making a single tree bear a variety of different kinds of fruit, even creating altogether new species by means of grafting – all these have been attempted at one time or another, occasionally with success. The notion of being able to play God with vegetable matter is obviously appealing.

One of the earliest extant gardening guides in English, a small anonymous 'tretice' that survives in a delightfully titled collection of fifteenth-century prose and poetry called the Porkington Manuscript, is mainly devoted to adventures in grafting. That most of its suggestions are cockeyed and clearly unlikely to work fails to diminish their charm. For example, we are told that you can get blue fruit by boring a hole 'near the root, even to the pith of the tree', filling it almost full with 'azure of Almayne' (presumably blue dye from Germany) and stopping it up with a wooden pin. Then you apply a poultice of moist earth and wrap the place with linen cloth, whereupon 'that fruit schal be of blewe colour'. In rather the same spirit, the treatise also explains how to grow cherries without stones, peaches whose stones contain nuts (graft a 'sprynge' of a peach tree on to the stock of a nut tree) and how to make a peach tree bear pomegranates by spraying it regularly with goat's milk.

One thing the Porkington Manuscript neglects to mention, perhaps because any serious amateur of the art would already know about it, is the idea of grafting a number of different varieties on to a single tree to produce what go-ahead American nurserymen nowadays call a 'fruit salad tree' and recommend for small gardens. Provided the stock is a suitable match for the scions – usually a related example of the same species – the practice is perfectly plausible, if whimsical. A citrus version might have lemons, limes, grapefruit and various kinds of oranges, a peach version apricots, plums, and nectarines. In the past apples were the favourite multiples, with grafters contending to see how many different kinds they could attach. As a boy in a Michigan orchard in the 1860s the great American horticulturist Liberty Hyde Bailey boasted that he had succeeded in grafting forty different apples on one tree. I considered this feat to be extremely impressive until I heard about the achievements of one

Haji Kaleem-Ullah Khan, who lives in a village near Lucknow in India and specializes in growing mangoes. Over the course of a number of years, Khan has grafted no less than 315 varieties of mango, including Tota, Alphonso, Neelam, Roomani, Ameer Pasand and Banganapalle, on a single seventy-five-year-old tree. The tree is still in good health, as is Khan.

Appropriately, given the contemporary interest in artificiality in garden design, the early years of Victoria's reign saw a boom in the more bizarre aspects of grafting. In *Victorian Gardens* Brent Elliott notes the enthusiasm with which professionals adopted the practice 'to demonstrate their authority over the merely natural' by, for example, grafting mistletoe on to oaks (a conjunction extremely rare in nature). William Barron, head gardener at Elvaston Castle near Derby and a master of grafting and topiary, turned his domain into what Elliott calls 'a grafter's playground', with an avenue of grafted cedars and other conifers. Famed for his ability to move large living trees, Barron also gained the awed admiration of mid-Victorian garden writers for grafting branches of weeping beech onto fully-grown normal trees to produce drooping mop-top crowns high above the ground.

Probably the most controversial piece of nineteenth-century grafting had nothing to do with showing off or reaching for weird effects. What it did was to challenge, in a startling way, the most basic assumption about the grafting process itself, and in turn long-held theories about reproduction.

Sometime in 1825 or 1826, a French nurseryman named Jean-Louis Adam set out to produce a 'standard' specimen of broom, grafting a bud of purple broom (*Cytisus purpureus*) on a stem of common laburnum (*Laburnum anagyroides*). The idea was to have a tuft of purple broom growing from a clear stem, rather the way standard roses are 'top worked' on a strong stem of multiflora or other stock. Now a standard broom may or may not

Modern botanists, with their far more sophisticated understanding of plant physiology than existed in the nineteenth century, are quite prepared to accept the reality of deliberate graft-hybrids (now generally called graft-chimeras after the lion-headed, goat-bodied, snake-tailed monster of Greek legend). They remain extremely rare, although a few others have turned up among the millions of grafts made by nurserymen, farmers and gardeners every year. A famous one occurred in Florence in 1674 when a scion of sour orange was grafted on to a seedling stock of citron to produce a presumably inedible chimera known as the Bizzarria orange. In 1904 a Williams Bon Chretien pear grafted on to quince stock resulted in a hybrid named +*Pyrocydonia*, which seems to have little to recommend it except its rarity. More common are those chimeras originating as spontaneous mutations or 'sports' – many variegated plants fall into this category.

Grafting, meanwhile, remains a pleasant and practical activity, so long as you don't try to create blue cherries or put a weeping willow on top of a Lombardy poplar. And it may be best to leave the mangoes to Haji Khan.

The Chinese Garden

There cannot be many among us who have had their own Chinese garden. In fact, these days not many Chinese have a Chinese garden. I had one once.

It was forty years ago, in Hong Kong. As a journalist working for a notoriously open-handed American magazine, I was able to rent, thanks to subsidies, a wonderful old mansion on the far side of Hong Kong Island. It had high ceilings with those hanging fans that go gently thunk-thunk as they turn, tall French windows, verandas wrapped around both floors, and a garden. It even had a gardener.

The gardener's name was Yang and he spoke no known dialect, which rather inhibited my learning anything about his craft even if I had been interested in horticulture, which I then wasn't. It seemed to me that he spent most of his time squatting on the lawn behind the house prodding weeds out of it with a nail. What I failed to note, and until now have failed to credit, was his expertise with potted plants. Scarcely a week went by without yet another wonderful new display of living flowers along the steps and balustrades of the house. Yang obviously knew what he was doing.

Because potted plants, I learn from this beautiful book by the late Maggie Keswick, are an essential element in Chinese gardening.* They are moveable, easily changed, and practical to maintain. Where you will not find a shrub border, a Jekyllian sweep of perennial or for that matter a lawn (ours was a concession to the round-eye owners of the house), you will always find potted plants – chrysanthemums, dwarf trees, cymbidium orchids. Along, of course, with a host of stranger (to us) features – bizarre rocks, a vast range of garden buildings from libraries to memorial temples and pavilions, artificial mountains, stagnant ponds and bits of poetry inscribed in the best calligraphy on practically everything.

The Chinese Garden, first published in 1978 (in a far more austere form than the present gloriously illustrated and revised edition), remains the best available account of the style and aesthetics of Chinese gardening. Much of this will always seem deeply foreign, especially to Western gardeners. For example, Keswick points out that the Chinese phrase for making a garden is 'digging ponds and piling mountains' – nothing about laying out beds or crossing gazanias. Horticulture is far less important than architecture; we plant a garden where a Chinese garden is built. And though a Chinese garden might well be beautiful, its basic purpose was not simply to charm or delight but to serve as a place for 'social and literary gatherings'.

Nothing shows the difficulty of grasping what Chinese designers were up to than their love for weird rocks. I'm sure I speak for many Western tourists visiting the gardens of the Summer Palace in Peking or the Ye Yuan in Shanghai when I say that I was not only bemused but slightly annoyed by the prominence given to a number of huge lumpy rocks full of holes. They looked as if they had been gnawed by some leviathan slug.

---

* *The Chinese Garden: History, Art and Architecture* by Maggie Keswick, edited by Alison Hardie (London 2003).

Thanks to Keswick, I now know that such stones have been the object of fascinated respect, even veneration, off and on for 2,000 years or more. Scholars wrote poems about them and gave them fancy names, emperors bankrupted themselves and their subjects collecting them. Really rare ones were even forged.

Fortunately you don't have to learn to admire Taihu stones to appreciate Chinese gardens, although these days the challenge may be greater on the ground than in books. Pavilions made out of cast concrete instead of delicately painted wood, bare electric light bulbs, narrow walkways choked with crowds of visitors, smelly ponds – these are the realities of many of the surviving famous gardens in China today. The scholars declaiming poems and singing in their arbours are long since departed.

Yet as *The Chinese Garden* makes plain, a vast amount of beauty and interest lives on in the tradition. The precise colour to paint a wall, so that the shadows of bamboo fluttering against it are seen to best advantage; the shape of a cut-out gate, calculated for lightness and the view beyond; bridges and latticework and pebble paths; above all the elusive balance to be achieved between the natural and the man-made – such matters as these are the concern of a Chinese garden maker. His ultimate aims are certainly familiar enough. 'If a home has not a garden and an old tree, I see not whence the everyday joys of life are to come,' wrote Chen Haozi in 1688.

I suppose it might be said that my gardener Yang, dealing with that dismal lawn, hadn't much of a chance, anyway. I don't know what happened to him, but the house and the garden, such as it was, has been swept away. Pleasant antiquities generally are in Hong Kong. A very posh block of flats now stands on the spot.

Manure

Ruth Stout, the doyenne of labour-free gardening, once observed that 'no poet I've ever heard of has written an ode to a load of manure'. I find this sad. To a gardener, there is nothing either funny or embarrassing about manure. On the contrary, we lust after it. We revel in dung.

No doubt non-gardeners, whose sensibilities tend to be more delicate, may find this strange. The smell and the general bad reputation of manure can be off-putting. Very little thought is required, however, to convince any rational person that manure represents an important and admirable phase in the Great Cycle of Nature. Besides, we would not love it so much if our plants did not love it more.

Gardening in the country, I have become a thoroughgoing coprophile. By now I've employed most kinds of manure, although I draw the line at night soil. The experience of living downwind of a large truck garden in Hong Kong, put me off that particular variety. That's not to say that I deny its efficacy, of course. The lettuces were sensational, even though you did have to douse them in potassium permanganate before consumption.

My sheep-farming neighbour in Wales used to turn up each spring with an offer of a trailer-load (or two, or three) of sheep manure, accumulated in his barn during lambing time. (The ewes had to be brought indoors for the big event, and the result, along with the lambs, was a lot of strawy manure.) I normally used this as an encourager for making compost or leaf mould. It was rather green and wet and fragrant, and not really aged enough to put directly on to the borders, so I customarily tossed a forkful or two between layers of leaves and hay. After ten months or so I had a sweet-smelling heap of lovely crumbly black stuff ready to be scumbled through a 1-inch wire mesh.

I'm still making this compost (what better to do with leaves?) but I had to move on from sheep manure when my neighbour gave up on sheep. His decision was understandable, given the vagaries of ovine midwifery – lambs tend to be born at 3:30am and to need help, and this goes on for weeks on end. Searching for another source of manure, I found myself the beneficiary – possibly the only happy one in Wales, if not all of Great Britain – of the great Foot and Mouth catastrophe of 2001. The few cattle farmers in our neighbourhood whose herds had escaped the prophylactic slaughter and incineration had ended up with a lot of quarantined animals that couldn't be moved or sold. They simply stood around in confined spaces producing manure. Small heaps gradually turned into mountains that nobody wanted – except me.

The cow manure was better than the sheep manure. It was already partly rotted, and though there was a lot of straw in it (it was still a bit 'long', as the saying goes), it had already pretty much stopped smelling. The farmer was so eager to get rid of it that he voluntarily brought out a tractor with a front-loader to save me having to fork it myself. I got what I thought would be a couple years' supply, and used it all in twelve months.

My most recent acquisition in the manure line is a handsome stack of well-rotted horse dung. This came from another neighbour, who raises blackcurrants and dresses his bushes with manure collected from stables in the area. His idea of a modest dungheap is a vast mound 15 feet high and about 40 feet across. My abstraction (with permission, of course) of a few petty trailer loads hardly made a dent.

Now this is truly beautiful stuff, and while admiring my pile it occurred to me that though I've tried out more different kinds than most people, I don't really know very much about manure. Old time garden guides were much more specific in spelling out its virtues and drawbacks than they are now, no doubt because dung was something a good deal harder to avoid in the days before the advent of the internal combustion engine. For example, I recall being mystified by a suggestion in an old book that 'road scrapings' were just the thing for asparagus. It took me a while to figure out that the reference was to horse droppings, not gravel.

As with many other things I'd like to know more about, however, manure turns out to be a complicated subject. A lot of chemistry is involved. Having failed freshman chemistry many years ago, I hesitate to do more than dance round the details, yet on the basis of an extremely amateur reading of several encyclopedia articles and heavy-duty manuals on organic gardening, I now know a few interesting facts:

• Sheep manure has more of all of the three important nutritive elements – nitrogen, potassium and phosphorus – than either cow or horse manure. But chicken manure has still more – twice as much nitrogen, three times as much potassium – as sheep manure. It is, in other words, 'hot'.

• Horse manure breaks down most quickly and thus makes its nutrients more quickly available to plants. Cow manure is slow to decay; it becomes sticky and compact and is more poorly distributed in the soil than horse dung. Sheep manure likewise. But these may be better to use where slow-acting agents are preferable, for example around fruit trees.

• Fresh manure should be spread and dug in in the autumn; rotted manure in the spring. Generally it is best to let manure rot (ferment, decay, compost – terminology seems flexible) thoroughly; what's left is pound-for-pound richer in available nutrients and they aren't so likely to 'burn' tender growth. Nicer to handle, too. Poultry manure is especially dangerous to use neat on growing plants because it is so powerful.

• Cover your dung heap with earth or a tarpaulin while it's rotting. One experiment showed that a pile of farmyard manure left exposed for twelve months lost nearly all of its soluble nitrogen and 78.2 per cent of other soluble minerals.

• Be patient – tests have demonstrated that relatively little of the nitrogen in farmyard manure is taken up by plants during the first year after application. On the other hand, manure's beneficent effects can be wonderfully lasting. One famous long-term test conducted over a period of nearly sixty years during the nineteenth century at Rothamsted established that as much as twenty years after ceasing to manure long-treated fields, crops were still showing the benefits. One reason, of course, is that the great virtue of manure lies as much – or more – in improving soil quality (drainage, water-holding capacity, texture) as in providing nutrients.

• Unrotted horse manure is especially full of weed seeds; unrotted cow and sheep manure somewhat less so, because these animals digest their food more completely. But any manure (except possibly pig manure), even rotted, will have a depressing number of weed seeds. More heat is required to kill them than is usually produced by the rotting of an ordinary dung heap.

In spite of the seeds and other minor drawbacks, everything one reads about manure suggests that we gardeners are perfectly right to be so enamoured of it. As the agricultural chemist John Augustus Voelker observed a century ago, 'the real difficulty with ı-yard manure is to get enough of it'. I can't help but agree. Artificial fertilizers just don't have the same cachet, and nothing inclines me to fall back upon some of the other substitutes recommended in the days before Monsanto and Dow got going. According to various helpful sources, these included fish, soot, 'graves' or candlemakers' refuse, hair, feathers, pond mud, and blubber ('found to produce very satisfactory results on beans, potatoes and other root crops'). In the meantime I'm still looking around for some chicken manure to experiment with. I have yet to run across anybody with a pig, so that will have to wait.

In the Tsangpo Gorges

The south-eastern corner of Tibet, where the Himalayas crumple into several tremendous ranges of peaks sliced through by river gorges, must be one of the strangest places on earth. It is certainly among the most difficult to get into and travel through, since a good bit of the topography is vertical. Its fascination does not lie simply in its remoteness, however. Boasting everything from virtually impenetrable rainforest jungles full of leeches and rhododendrons to temperate forests to bare alpine screes, it is the home of a vast number of plant species, many of which have been successfully introduced to Western gardens. Even today, it is still yielding unknown varieties.

The combination of geographical mysteries and what has been called 'an almost inconceivable wealth of flora' proved irresistible to a number of explorers and plant-hunters over the last century, above all the redoubtable Frank Kingdon Ward. Beginning in 1910 and continuing for forty-five years, Ward repeatedly trekked into the region and the adjoining Chinese and Burmese territories collecting dozens of rhododendrons and other shrubs, as well as primulas, lilies, gentians and – most famous of all – the blue poppy *Meconopsis betonicifolia*. In between trips, moreover, he wrote, producing over two dozen books about plants and about his journeys. The best of these, describing a year-long expedition undertaken in 1924–5 with a decidedly unbotanical Scottish gentleman named Lord Cawdor, is *The Riddle of the Tsangpo Gorges*.*

The riddle was this: The biggest river in Tibet is the Tsangpo (Zangbo in the modern Chinese spelling), which flows from west to east just north of the Himalayas. The biggest river south of the Himalayas, in eastern India, is the Brahmaputra. By the 1920s, thanks to the largely unsung labours of several native spy-surveyors dispatched by the Survey of India and the daring of a couple of young British officers exploring more or less on their own, it was generally accepted that the two rivers were one. Somehow or other, this great torrent managed to cut its way in deep gorges clear through the 25,000-foot Himalaya wall, descending from an altitude of about 10,000 feet in Tibet to less than 2,000 where it emerged in the placid lowlands of Assam, some 100 miles further on. Given the scale of the drop, was it not possible, indeed probable, that the unexplored gorges hid waterfalls as big as Niagara or Victoria?

Some people were sure it did. The geographer Sir Thomas Holdich, obviously untrammelled by any personal experience, called the putative falls 'stupendous' and suggested that it would not be long before there was 'a spacious hotel for sightseers and sportsmen' overlooking them. Others, particularly those who had tried and failed to follow the course of the river through the gorges, recognized that even finding out whether the falls existed was a terrible challenge. For long stretches the river flowed completely out of sight between sheer walls of rock a mile or more deep.

It would be pleasant to report that Ward and Cawdor braved the hazards and discovered the giant waterfalls. They didn't,

---

* *Frank Kingdon Ward's Riddle of the Tsangpo Gorges* edited by Kenneth Cox (London 2001).

exactly – what they found instead, on the unmapped section of the river that they for the first time perilously managed to see, was a number of lower cascades and cataracts. This led them to conclude that there were no truly big falls, and later explorers have pretty much agreed. But the lack of a clincher does nothing to subtract from the charm and fascination of Ward's book, now reprinted in a gloriously illustrated, updated, and expensive edition.

I don't pretend to be completely objective – I've prized a copy of the original 1926 printing (which coincidentally bears the bookplate of another great plant-hunter, Joseph Rock of tree peony fame) for many years – but for anyone even remotely interested in plants, adventure, and the romance of blank spots on the map, *The Riddle of the Tsangpo Gorges* is irresistable. Ward is a crisp and evocative writer, and a first-rate phrase-maker. The high plateau is 'all dust and ice and a raving wind'; rhododendrons in bloom on the Doshong La resemble 'a tidal wave of tense colours which gleam and glow in leagues of breaking light'; the sky at 8,000 feet is 'an aching blue'. When he describes the climate of Assam as 'eight months wet and four months damned wet', you can almost feel the rain trickling down your neck.

Just how hazardous the trip was comes across vividly. Scaling cliffs and negotiating flimsy rope bridges sounds bad enough, but as we learn from a new introduction written by Ward's widow, he apparently suffered seriously from acrophobia (as well as a fear of snakes). The most interesting new plants, moreover, generally seemed to be growing halfway up terrifying precipices. Then there was the basic problem of collecting seed. Identifying a rarity in bloom was only half the game – you had to mark it and come back later after the seed had ripened. In Ward's case this sometimes meant digging through several feet of snow while avalanches threatened, or clambering up an ice-covered rock face in hopes (frequently disappointed) of finding a still-intact seed capsule on a prize rhododendron.

With few exceptions, only in the last decade has it been possible for Western explorers to penetrate the gorges and build on Ward's and Cawdor's discoveries. Accounts of these recent findings are an extra attraction of the new edition, along with a plethora of beautifully reproduced photographs of plants and landscape. They make brilliantly clear that the passage of seventy-five years has not brought a lot of change to this dangerous and mysterious corner of the world. It is still intensely primitive and scarcely inhabited. In 1997, however, one expedition was startled to find a labour gang digging a ditch along a steep mountainside not far from the gorges. It was, they were told, for a fibre optic cable installation.

PLANTERS AND
PLANTSMEN

Commerson's Secret

There's nothing easy about being a serious plant hunter, but at least you have the prospect of becoming famous for the plants you find. Philibert Commerson was exceptionally serious, suffering all sorts of disasters in the service of his trade, and has every right to be renowned for his achievements. After all, they included the discovery of the bougainvillea. So there must be a sort of celestial injustice in the fact that today Commerson has been thoroughly upstaged in the fame stakes by his valet, who probably never discovered anything at all. This is the unlikely story.

Philibert Commerson was born in 1727 in a backward, swampy part of France called the Dombes. Fascinated from boyhood by natural history, he decided while still studying law at Montpellier to become a botanist. It was an era of botanical excitement. Great botanic gardens were being built all over Europe; Linnaeus himself was developing his binomial system in Uppsala; new plants were flowing into Europe at an unprecedented rate.

Being a man of somewhat violent enthusiasm, Commerson decided to create his own private herbarium, and set about collecting with a vigor that soon got him into trouble. Montpellier possessed an excellent botanic garden. Its superintendent was the professor of botany himself, a grand and not particularly accommodating figure, especially when he discovered that Commerson was filching specimens without permission. For a young scholar intending to enter the field, this was a bad move. When he took a fruit of a desert weed called *Réaumuria* ('I left him two,' Commerson protested), the professor permanently barred him from access to the garden. This destroyed any possibility of an academic botanical career. Commerson fumed – his self-justifying letters are pungent with attacks on Professor Sauvages. But the contretemps spurred him to even greater collecting exertions in central France and the Alps. Near drowning, falls from precipices, avalanches, even rabies (self-treated – he now had a medical degree) all failed to put a stop to what he called his 'botanomania'.

Commerson was not one to linger in obscurity. He was soon involved in the development of several new botanic gardens, in his spare time meeting and corresponding with other leading naturalists. Marriage brought him briefly to rest as a doctor in a small Burgundian town, but within two years his much-loved young wife was dead in childbirth, plunging him into deep despair. 'Governed by a spirit of darkness and discord,' as he put it in a letter, he gloomily concentrated on his studies. These apparently included writing a vast comprehensive catalogue – never, needless to say, published – drawing together everything known about all three branches of natural history: animal, vegetable and mineral. Eventually, however, he yielded to the persuasion of friends, moving to Paris, joining the active scientific community there and leaving his son Archambault to be raised by relatives.

Commerson's energy and ambition soon brought him to the attention of the government and offered him the prospect of adventure on a larger scale than he had found heretofore. The 1760s were not a happy time for French imperialists; France had just lost Canada on the Plains of Abraham, and other countries were busily claiming territories in far corners of the globe. At this juncture came a proposal from the brilliant Louis Antoine de Bougainville, soldier, mathematician, diplomat and all-round hero, to mount a voyage of exploration around the world, possibly picking up a colony or two along the way. The royal government bit eagerly, providing two ships and funds for staffing. Commerson was offered the post of naturalist.

To a man like him, the assignment was irresistible. It brought with it not only a title – Botaniste Naturaliste du Roi – but an unrivalled opportunity to collect unknown specimens. He promptly wrote a will giving, among other dispositions, his body to science and a modest legacy to his housekeeper. Then he raced off to Rochefort to take ship. He was joined there by his valet, a slight young man named Bonnefoy.

The circumnavigation, which lasted more than two years, proved to be something less than successful for De Bougainville, who founded no new colonies and missed discovering Australia by a matter of a few miles. But it was all that Commerson could have hoped. 'A single hunt, one fishing expedition, or a simple stroll,' he wrote from South America, 'makes me a sort of Midas, in whose hands everything becomes golden. I often do not know where to begin.' In Brazil he first came upon bougainvillea, described it and named it along with dozens of other less famous species, working frantically in his usual fashion to keep abreast of the tide of fresh discoveries. At one point De Bougainville had to confine him to his cabin to give a dangerous sore on his leg time to heal; the naturalist was inclined to ignore anything as trivial as incipient gangrene.

The expedition made its way south through the Straits of Magellan, where Commerson collected more plants and birds, and out into the Pacific. Fish were his interest here, both for eating and dissection. Helped by his 'indefatigable' valet Bonnefoy (who became known as his 'beast of burden'), he busily drew, described and then packed up specimens for eventual shipment to Paris. Two collections of plants and one of fish had already gone back from Rio (half the plants never arrived); now Commerson's quarters were filling up again with bales and boxes.

It was in Tahiti that one of the most extraordinary discoveries of the entire expedition was made, a discovery that had nothing to do with plants, birds or fish. It concerned Commerson's handsome young valet, his 'beast of burden'. There had already been, among the crew, some suspicions about the boy. Why, for example, had he always avoided being seen undressed? Why was his voice so high-pitched? The answer was a shocking affront to naval regulations. Some Tahitians spotted Bonnefoy bathing by himself and revealed all. As De Bougainville later reported it in his journal: 'With tears in her eyes, Baré [Bonnefoy] confessed that she was a girl and that she had fooled her master [Commerson] by presenting herself dressed as a man in Rochefort at the moment of sailing. . . . She is neither ugly nor beautiful and no more than twenty-five years old.' She claimed to be an orphan impoverished in a lawsuit and had disguised herself in order to make the journey around the world; the prospect of such an adventure 'piqued her curiosity'.

De Bougainville was inclined to be forgiving in spite of the affront to regulations. He admired her resolution. And she had, after all, been very useful as an assistant to Commerson. What he officially did not know, and research has only recently revealed, is that she was more than merely useful. She was the housekeeper mentioned in Commerson's will. She and the naturalist had been living together as man and wife for three or four years prior to the voyage. She had even borne him a child, whose death probably provided the incentive for her stratagem.

It must have been quite a relief to Jeanne to have at least part of her secret out in the open, although it is hard to believe that De Bougainville did not guess the whole truth. No doubt he chivalrously ignored it. In any case, after leaving Tahiti conditions aboard ship became extremely difficult – scurvy, near starvation, bad water. The botanizing and collecting nevertheless went on apace. De Bougainville narrowly missed Australia, went through the New Hebrides and Solomons and on into Indonesia, and finally crossed the Indian Ocean to Isle de France (Mauritius), already a French possession. At the welcome request of a scientifically inclined governor, Commerson chose to stay, to put his collections in order and explore the natural wonders of the island. Jeanne, naturally, stayed with him.

This should have been a happier time, and in some ways seems to have been. He developed a botanic garden, explored the flora and fauna of Mauritius, and travelled to Isle de Bourbon (Réunion) and Madagascar, always finding and recording new species. 'The limits of Natural History have been pushed back by my own observations,' he later wrote with some accuracy, 'twice as far as they were beforehand.' But his health was bad, and political squabbles resulted in his being dismissed from his post as naturalist. Infuriated, he vowed to keep working, and did so in his usual hard-driving way. He was too ill; on 13 March 1773, at the age of only forty-six, he died.

And Jeanne Baré (Baret or Barret – the spelling varies), the loyal housekeeper/valet/wife? Left nearly penniless, she managed to open a *cabaret-billard* in St Louis, the capital of Mauritius, and within a year had married a French soldier and returned to France, thus completing her trip around the world. Nothing is known of any continuing interest in botany, but at her death she willed all her goods to Commerson's heirs. Commerson had done his best to immortalize her by naming a South American plant (reportedly of ambiguous gender) *Baretia bonnafidia*, but it is now known as *Turrea heterophylla*.

In recent years, interest in feminist history has brought retrospective fame to Baré as the first woman to circle the globe. There are nearly a thousand times more Internet references to her than there are to Philibert Commerson.

Christo

There are those who maintain that the late Christopher Lloyd, Christo to his many friends, was the best gardener of his time. I'm not sure I wouldn't go along with that judgement. It's difficult to think of any real competitors. In more than a dozen books and innumerable magazine and newspaper columns, and above all in his 5½-acre garden at Great Dixter in East Sussex, Lloyd proved over and over that he not only knew more about horticulture than almost anyone else, but was also prepared to learn more – to experiment, challenge, break rules.

It was hardly the season for garden visiting on the January day I drove down to Dixter to see him. There were sheets of rain and a 60mph gale was blowing, rattling the ancient windows of the sitting room in the grand medieval house. Trees were falling all over the south-east of England but Lloyd was nonchalant. 'This is a garden of hedges – and anyway all the trees blew down in '87.' In fact Dixter does have trees, plenty of them. But its hedges, marvellous sculptured yews mostly planted by Lloyd's father Nathaniel before World War I, are rightly more famous. Dividing and structuring the gardens laid out by the architect Sir Edwin Lutyens when he restored the house, they furnish a particularly powerful presence in the depths of winter.

Christopher Lloyd was at the time of my visit approaching

eighty-three, a stocky, somewhat stooped figure who plodded in a determined fashion through the house and gardens as if he were thirty years younger. A coronary bypass operation a few years previously slowed him a bit, according to friends, but only superficially. There was no suggestion that he was going to yield to the demands of age. He had every right to: every week since 1963 he had written a gardening column for *Country Life*, along with a second weekly column for the *Guardian* and other articles for a variety of publications. And he always had a book going, even though he was able to concentrate on it only in the winter; summer was too full of gardening, friends visiting, and expeditions to the opera at Glyndeborne. His last book, called *Succession Planting for Adventurous Gardeners*, was his fifteenth.

As the wind howled in the chimney, we sat on a sofa in front of a big fireplace stoked with seasoned logs cut in the estate wood. Between us, under a blanket, lay one of Lloyd's two beloved dachshunds, Dahlia, now sixteen years old, blind and very frail. The other one of his 'horticultural dogs', Canna (only six or seven – 'a puppy') soon pushed open the door and came in to join us. Lloyd chose the names, he says, because 'they are easy to say or to shout or to speak caressingly'. Then after a moment, he observes: 'Yucca would be a good name.'

It is no wonder that Lloyd's thoughts tended to run on horticultural lines. Gardening had been a major part of his life since he was a boy. Both his father and mother were experts – his father wrote a book on topiary – and he grew up with a love of plants in his blood. Yet his career as a gardener was hardly straightforward. Leaving Rugby to go to university, a counsellor advised him to take up architecture, whereupon he spent a few miserable months learning that he had no talent in this line at all. Switching to modern languages, he spent a year or two at Cambridge before entering the army early in World War II. Five years of service in an artillery regiment followed for 'Gunner Surveyor Lloyd', during which he narrowly missed seeing action in the Far East; the Japanese surrendered as he was *en route* to Rangoon from Africa. Demobbed, he found himself at loose ends and without a lot of confidence in his future. 'I had a pretty low opinion of myself at the end of the war,' he told me.

What saved him was gardening – serious gardening. Turning down an offered place at Cambridge, he went instead to Wye College, the agriculture sciences branch of University College London, and with success and satisfaction took a degree in horticulture. The subject so suited him that upon graduation he was offered the post of assistant lecturer in decorative horticulture. For four years he taught at Wye, until what he terms a 'disagreement' with the departmental head caused him to make another key decision: to return to Great Dixter, set up a nursery for clematis and rare plants, and garden. That was in 1954 and fifty years later he is still here.

In those fifty years a good deal has changed at Great Dixter – and a good deal more has remained the same. The original Lutyens layout of the gardens remains almost unaltered, apart from a few details (Lloyd's father created the Sunk Garden, with its pool, after World War I), a situation which Lloyd was happy to accept. 'I'm definitely not a garden designer,' he said adamantly. 'Dixter is so well designed that there is no reason to change it.'

The plantings, on the other hand, were in an almost constant state of flux. It was Lloyd's delight to consider and reconsider, often with startling results, virtually every aspect of the plantings of every bed. For schemes to be repeated year after year would be regarded, one suspects, as something of a defeat. His most famous revolutionary gesture, among many, was to pull almost all of the roses out of Lutyens's classic rose garden, replacing them with such un-British species as hardy bananas and cannas, thereby achieving considerable outraged publicity and a stunning, much-imitated new feature. (Lloyd in fact had nothing against roses – he still had more than a hundred bushes scattered in other beds – but 'replant disease' made it progressively more difficult to replaced aged specimens in the old bed.) The Rose Garden is now the Exotic Garden.

Such bold gestures were a Lloyd trademark. 'He kept pushing out the boundaries,' says Mary Keen, a leading English garden designer and writer. 'He was never afraid to try things, and if they didn't work, why, he just tried something else.' His iconoclasm might have to do with colour ('Actually, I have a sneaking affection for magenta, in the right circumstances') or with texture and shape ('I love the bumpiness of my plantings') or with the choice of plant materials ('Bedding out [appeals] because of the frequently repeated opportunities it gives me of trying out different plants, new textures and, above all, new colour schemes'). His books and articles were filled with pleas against complacency ('Even shrubs should be put through the hoop at regular intervals') and support for adventurousness ('The best gardening is experimental as well as ephemeral').

What this meant at Great Dixter was a sense of real excitement. The grand lines of the gardens laid out ninety years ago may still exist but within them, as if on a kind of giant easel, Lloyd worked endless changes. Was this simply the result of a low boredom threshold? Mary Keen thinks not. 'Christo was a very very intelligent man, an artist, and this was his art form. He broke the mould – and we all followed.'

In practical terms, the style of gardening followed at Great Dixter was extremely high-maintenance. Bedding might be renewed during the summer as many as three times to ensure maximum effect, which required bringing along many plants in reserve. Lupins, for example, 'hideous passengers for the rest of the summer after their early June flowering', might be treated as biennials and replaced immediately with tithonia or China asters; meanwhile next year's lupins, started from seed in April, grew on elsewhere. It was, as fellow garden writer Stephen Anderton observes, 'a very hardworking garden'.

That Lloyd was able to carry out such demanding schemes, and indeed to keep Dixter going as an active and lively operation, he gratefully credited to the presence of a young man named Fergus Garrett. Garrett bore the title of Head Gardener; he has been in fact much more a sort horticultural major-domo cum strong right hand to Lloyd, supervising the garden staff, doing the trickiest bits of physical labour, talking over what needed to be done and seeing that it is accomplished. 'I can't be a very active gardener anymore,' Lloyd admitted, 'but I try to spend each Thursday morning with Fergus studying one particular section of the garden and what might improve it.' Garrett came up with many ideas and could probably run the place himself. But as Lloyd remarked, 'He never does anything without telling me first. He knows Dixter is mine.'

Lloyd's existence was obviously greatly eased by Garrett. 'Fergus is a great prop,' he said admiringly. Fergus helped Lloyd develop ideas for columns and managed arrangements for trips such as the one they made together to America in 2003 – Vancouver, Seattle, Denver and Chicago – with Lloyd giving lectures all along the way. Lloyd was incidentally very fond of Americans. He found them 'very stimulating, and much more open than we are. And they are willing to pay, which the English aren't.' During recent years he ran an annual week-long 'school' for American gardeners who paid a fee to come to Great Dixter. They worked in the gardens, listened to lectures and watched demonstrations. 'They have a fine time,' he said. 'Some have come two or three times.' The last night was marked by a big dinner in the hall, after which Lloyd read them a ghost story by Saki.

According to Anderton, one reason that Lloyd has been so influential, apart from his writings, was his 'incredible generosity with his time and his willingness to welcome visitors to Great Dixter'. He clearly enjoyed company, especially young people, and there were usually a fair number around. His Who's Who entry listed 'entertaining and cooking for friends' among his recreations, although the days when he would get up at 5am to cook for a houseful of guests were past. He could still rustle up a delicious lunch (for me he produced leeks, Pink Fir Apple potatoes, sea bass fillets and a bottle of Riesling, topped off with the last of the season's pears with dried cranberries and chopped preserved ginger), but the scale is necessarily diminished. Getting old, he confessed, was a nuisance. 'It's embarrassing. But everyone around me is very kind.' One recourse, which he employed for many years, was the impromptu nap. A friend who went on a trip to South Africa with him a few years ago tells how at the end of an elegant lunch with a group of local luminaries in Cape Town, Lloyd allowed as how he would like his nap. Much talk of getting him a bedroom. 'No, never mind,' he said, 'it's fine right here.' So with a couple of dozen people swirling around he did his twenty minutes and was ready to go again.

One thing that mellowed only a little with age was Lloyd's famously sharp tongue and impatience with what he saw as incompetence or indifferent thinking. This could be disconcerting, especially to the unprepared. After he had his bypass surgery, he decided that the time had come to go home, no matter what the hospital authorities had to say about it. Climbing out of bed, he dressed and announced 'Come on, Fergus, let's go,' leaving the clerk fruitlessly waving unsigned discharge forms. There is no doubt that Lloyd knew his mind. His writings, rich in strong opinions strongly and crisply expressed, make that plain.

Yet ready as he may have been to unsettle other people, he was not readily unsettled himself. The garden writer Anna Pavord tells a lovely story about travelling with Lloyd and Garrett in a remote region of Eastern Turkey while she was researching her book on tulips. They were suddenly stopped at a roadblock by what appeared to be heavily armed bandits. The situation was very tense. While Garrett, who is half Turkish, nervously negotiated with one of men and Pavord, terrified, figured their end had come, Lloyd simply sat gazing benignly on the scene. To the relief of Pavord and Garrett, they were finally allowed to proceed unharmed. Lloyd's only comment: 'What an interesting face that boy had.'

Although it is difficult to imagine Great Dixter without Christopher Lloyd, he was confident that 'the prospect for the gardens is good with Fergus'. Before his death he launched a charitable trust to run the place, and much preferred that it remain private, rather than going to English Heritage or the National Trust. 'But that won't be up to me.' In any case, its fame and popularity continue to increase. Last year nearly 50,000 paying visitors came to admire the old timber-framed house (most of which dates back to the fifteenth century) and the gardens, perhaps taking away a clematis or a shrub from the nursery, almost certainly taking away a few ideas about colour or texture or planting possibilities from the borders or the meadows.

I did myself. Just as I was leaving, the rain stopped and for a brief time the sun came out from behind the racing clouds. We walked out to see the one bit of the garden that was coming into bloom – the snowdrops along the side of the Barn Garden. These were the earliest varieties, Lloyd explained; others would follow, to make a constant progression of bloom for two months or more. I have snowdrops in my garden – most people do – but until now I had no idea that there were so many kinds or that they could bloom over such a long period. Thank you, Christo; we shall remember you.

Englebert Kaempfer and the Vegetable Lamb

In considering the exploits of the great plant hunters it's nice to think of the plants they hoped to find, but didn't. Reginald Farrer, for example, entertained an ambition to find a blue rhododendron. Although I cannot quite understand why they'd want one, a number of moderately sensible botanical explorers have searched for a black rose. Others have hunted fruitlessly for lost orchids or extinct ferns. Englebert Kaempfer looked for something even stranger, and was not very surprised when he didn't find it.

Strictly speaking, Kaempfer was not a plant hunter. At least he would not have called himself that, in spite of the fact that he was the very first Westerner to explore the flora of Japan. By profession he was actually a doctor, but you'd have to look a long time to find anybody as absolutely, ceaselessly curious about practically everything – not excepting plants – as Englebert Kaempfer.

He was born in the small town of Lemgo in northern Germany in 1651 and proved to be a brilliant student, collecting degrees in several subjects before settling down to serious study of 'physick' and natural history. He might have found a lucrative post in one of a number of courts, but, consumed by wanderlust, chose instead to join a Swedish embassy to the King of Persia. His route took him through Russia and across the Caspian Sea (where he nearly drowned in an unexpected storm), with the many delays for diplomatic negotiations spent investigating natural phenomena and noting unfamiliar plants. When the embassy concluded, he wasn't ready to go home. Instead, he signed on as chief surgeon to the Dutch East India fleet, which offered the prospect of a journey much further east and, ultimately, an extended visit to that most mysterious country, Japan.

Kaempfer, as one early biographer observed, had all the qualifications for a good botanist. These included 'a body inured to hardships, a great stock of industry and application and . . . an excellent hand at drawing'. Considering his achievements in Japan, the praise was warranted. Conditions were exceptionally difficult. The Dutch, the only Europeans allowed into the country, were confined to a tiny artificial island in Nagasaki Bay except for a once-yearly tribute mission to the shogun's court in Edo (now Tokyo). With typical enterprise, Kaempfer managed not only to collect material for a monumental history of Japan, but to examine and draw – in exquisite detail – dozens of hitherto unknown plants, from rhododendrons to the gingko tree. During his two-year stay (1690–2) he even succeeded in establishing a botanic garden inside the main gate of the Dutch trading post, where he could study his finds with a scientific eye.

It is for his discoveries in Japan that Englebert Kaempfer will probably always be best known, and rightly so. For those of us with a taste for oddities, however, it may be worth recalling another of his botanical adventures, which he described in a fascinating book* that has only recently been translated from

---

* *Exotic Pleasures: Fascicle III, Curious Scientific and Medical Observations* by Englebert Kaempfer. Translation with an introduction and commentary by Robert W. Carrubba (Carbondale, Illinois 1996).

Latin for the first time. If nothing else, Kaempfer's dealings with the legendary plant/animal called the Borometz show vividly how the world of plant hunting has changed, and how the powerful scepticism of men like him raised modern science out of the dismal bog of medieval credulity.

The first mention of the Borometz, otherwise known as the Scythian Lamb or the Vegetable Lamb of Tartary, is lost in the distant past. Reports of the plant/beast were undoubtedly current by the fourteenth century; Sir John Mandeville mentions it in the course of describing more spectacular wonders such as headless men with eyes in their shoulders and gold mines operated by dog-sized ants. Unlike many of Mandeville's marvels, however, the Vegetable Lamb sounded plausible. After all, the kingdom of plants contains some pretty peculiar things. There are plants that eat insects, plants that register feeling, plants that can grow in boiling water and others that don't mind being frozen in ice. Why not, then, a plant that can grow into an animal, an animal, moreover, covered in the most delicate and valuable wool?

According to the best authorities, the Borometz grew from seed like that of a melon, 'only rounder'. The stalk sprang vertically from a rosette of leaves, eventually producing a sort of fruit or seed capsule that, when ripe, burst open to reveal a tiny lamb covered in 'very white' wool. As the lamb matured, it naturally needed to graze, so the stalk accommodatingly bent down, enabling the small animal to reach the surrounding grass. When the grass within reach was gone, that was the end of the Vegetable Lamb – unless, of course, it had already had the bad luck to fall victim to a wolf. Being composed of the actual flesh, blood and bone of a real lamb, it was said to be a favourite prey of wolves, though other carnivores, oddly, left it alone.

Certain Renaissance scholars gave a lot of thought to the Borometz, not that any of them had actually seen one. Claude

Duret devoted a whole chapter to it in his *Histoire Admirable des Plantes*, coming up with what he claimed to be a thousand-year-old reference in the Talmud. In the 1520s, one Sigismund, Baron von Herberstein, took time off from a diplomatic mission to Russia to make enquiries and came away convinced that the Borometz existed. 'It had a head, yes, ears, and all other parts of a newly born lamb . . . although I had previously regarded these Borametz [the spelling varies] as fabulous, the accounts of it were confirmed to me by so many persons of credence that I thought it right to describe it.' (Clearly, the Baron hadn't seen one either.) A hundred years later another easily impressed traveller wandering the 'step' west of the Volga reported 'the Baromez or Barnitsch' growing on 'the great dry and waste heath'. It had, he said, 'a head, feet and tail' and was 'in appearance very much resembling a sheep'. Its stalk was 2½ feet high.

Now anything as unusual as this was bound to pique the curiosity of a man like Englebert Kaempfer, so when he found himself in Persia with time on his hands, he set out to find one. The search was an embarrassing flop. 'As I investigated to my humiliation and disgust,' he wrote later in *Amoenitates Exoticae* ('Exotic Pleasures'), he found that neither ordinary people or expert botanists 'anywhere in Tartaria' had any knowledge or record of the existence of such a thing. It was all 'pure fiction and fable'. In fact, 'nothing called Borometz (except for a herd of sheep) can be found in this area'. Kaempfer had gone straight to the heart of the mystery. The name of the creature had apparently originated in a linguistic blunder – *baran* or *barreh* was the word for sheep in Russian or Persian – while the legend itself, he argued, grew out of the local practice of using the expensive, finely furred skin of an unborn or newly-born Karakul lamb for trimming turbans and cloaks. 'I did not learn this truth from careless inquiry but from experience, the true teacher,' he declared stoutly.

Since Kaempfer's day, other theories debunking the Borometz legend have emerged, the most likely being that it was based on a fanciful description of a cotton plant. Yet some belief in the Vegetable Lamb lived on. In 1698, what purported to be a complete specimen arrived in London and was exhibited to the Royal Society by Sir Hans Sloan. It was woolly and had four legs. (An example may still be seen at the Museum of Garden History in London.) Sloan, however, was able to establish that this particular lamb had actually been carved out of the root of a large Oriental fern of an unknown species. Some years later, the fern was found and identified. Appropriately, as the closest living relative of a Vegetable Lamb, it received – and to this day bears – the name *Cibotium borametz*.

Losers

I lose things all the time, most usually my glasses. It doesn't much matter; they turn up; I can spare the time to hunt. But real loss can be a serious matter, the more so if your business is finding things – if you are, say, a plant hunter intent on collecting and introducing new species from some insalubrious part of the world.

The bitter truth of this struck me when I was reading about Thomas Coulter, the Irishman who first found the shrub with those lovely, silky, golden-hearted blossoms, *Romneya coulterii*. I had figured that his would be a good story; somewhere in the back of my mind I conflated him with the Coulter who famously ran six miles naked through prickly pears to escape a group of Blackfoot Indians intent on having, at the least, his scalp. As I soon found, however, the runner, John, had nothing to do with the plant collector, apart from near contemporaneity and the fact that they were both doing their things in Western America.

But Thomas was interesting too. Reading about his exploits – and for this the place to go, the only place, is a small privately-published volume called *A Man Who can Speak to Plants* by E. Charles Nelson and Alan Probert – I couldn't help being impressed by the multiplicity of his talents. Doctor, botanist, mining engineer, even amateur herpetologist (he kept snakes in his pockets and once shipped a crateful from France back to Ireland, where there aren't any, as 'a patriotic act'), he was as well prepared as any man in the 1820s to make some serious botanical discoveries.

As it turned out, Coulter's career as a full-time explorer and plant hunter was extremely short, scarcely more than a year from the time he left his post as physician and manager of silver and lead mines in Central Mexico. His main finds, notably the romneya, were made in Calfornia, mostly in the hostile back country along the coast between Monterey and the Mexican border. His health was poor, and it must have been with some relief that he finally packed up his dried specimens, his pine cones, his notebooks and journals and sketch maps, with the intention of returning home.

It is here that we arrive at the matter of losing things. For when the doughty engineer/botanist finally reached Ireland, having been briefly delayed by more mining business, doctoring and revolutionary chaos in Mexico, he learned to his horror that one of his precious cases, shipped with care across the Atlantic, had vanished *en route*. It was the case that contained, inevitably, Coulter's diaries and notebooks, and it was never seen again.

The loss must have been a considerable blow. Coulter spent the remainder of his fairly short life in a state of gloom in Dublin, arranging his herbarium, studying entomology and, curiously enough, target shooting – he was a crack shot. Yet it occurs to me that his depression might not have been so profound if he had known that in losing his precious manuscripts he was simply following in the footsteps of many other plant hunters, some of them far more cruelly handled by fate than he was. Coulter at least was left with a few wispy dried specimens of *Romneya coulterii* to finger when he was feeling particularly morose; they can still be found in the Trinity College Dublin Herbarium.

He might, for example, have contemplated the travails of David Douglas, whose intrepid forays in the American Northwest are legendary, and whom he had, incidentally, met and befriended in Monterey. The discoverer of hundreds of hitherto unknown species of conifers and herbaceous plants, from the Douglas fir (*Pseudotsuga menziesii*) to the California poppy (*Platystemon*), Douglas had a real knack for losing important objects. These included whole plant collections, often those assembled in extreme and painful circumstances. In 1826, he notes in his journal 'the nearly total loss of my collections crossing the River Sandiam' in what is now Oregon. The same thing happened a few years later when his canoe ran on to rocks and capsized while he was paddling down the Fraser River in British Columbia. On that occasion he lost 400 species of plants and all his field notes and journals. And if running water was a challenge to numerous plant hunters, relatively few of them can have been reduced by sheer hunger to eating a hard-won collection. Douglas and a companion named Mackenzie were. They once lost all their supplies during a crossing of the Columbia River, and after a couple of foodless days gave in and started munching. 'We used all the berries I had collected on the journey, and Mr Mackenzie suffered some inconvenience from having eaten a few roots of a species of *Narthecium*,' Douglas wrote dyspeptically.

Boats of all kinds seem to have posed a particular hazard. Robert Fortune, whose introductions from China in the mid-nineteenth century included such splendid garden standards as the Japanese anemone (*Anemone hupehensis* var. *japonica*) and *Weigela florida*, was caught in a typhoon between the Chinese mainland and Taiwan. The big blow lasted for three days, at the end of which Fortune considered himself lucky to have escaped with his life. Gone, however, were two glazed boxes containing the plants he had collected. This experience must have had an impact; when it came time later to send the rest of his botanical prizes back to England, he divided them between four separate vessels.

Quite apart from the near-hopeless problem of getting live plants back from distant places by sea (a difficulty eased only in the 1830s by Dr Thomas Ward's invention of the Wardian case), shipwreck put an end to a number of collections, if not collectors. The entire assemblage of Chinese plants gathered by Clarke Abel, the naturalist attached to Lord Amherst's 1816 mission to Peking, and his assistants ended up on a reef off the coast of Sumatra when HMS *Alceste* foundered on the return voyage. The experience of Joseph Rock was, if possible, still sadder. He laboured for years in West China collecting not only plants, birds and animals, but studying local languages and anthropology. When World War II started he was about to begin publishing his masterwork on the Na-khi people. Japanese bombs falling on the printworks in Shanghai destroyed the plates of the book. Then, fearful of what might happen to the rest of his notes and manuscripts – the work of twelve hard years – he packed them off to Europe by sea for safety. The ship carrying the papers was torpedoed; poor Rock spent the rest of his life trying to recall what he had written.

Still more exotic and unexpected disasters struck other plant hunters. George Forrest, whose discoveries in Szechuan and Yunnan so enriched our stock of rhododendrons (to say nothing of *Gentiana sino-ornata*, several extraordinary primulas and much more), unwittingly found himself in the middle of a sort of Tibetan jihad by infuriated monks against Catholic priests in the region. Numerous priests and local Christians were butchered; Forrest, starving and feverish, evaded capture for nearly two weeks before reaching safety. But he lost everything: 'nearly all the results of a whole season's work, a collection of most valuable plants numbering full 2,000 species, seeds of 80 species, and 100 photographic negatives. It is difficult,' he observed mournfully, 'to estimate the value of such a loss.'

Being Forrest, of course, he immediately set out to replace his losses, and did so with such success that a year later he could sail home with a full docket of new plants. As a collector in the employ of rich and eager patrons, moreover, there was no question of his finds being overlooked or badly handled when they finally got back. The botanist priest Jean-Marie Delavay, on the contrary, never even had the satisfaction (or rather pain) of knowing that many of his discoveries in West China, prepared and sent back to Paris with exemplary care and attention, were ultimately lost all over again; staff at the Musée d'Histoire Naturelle failed to propagate seeds or publish more than a few descriptions.

Delavay died on the battlefield, as it were; so did Reginald Farrer, whose collecting activities in the endless rain and fog of Upper Burma came to a sorry end when he was struck down by a fever. We will never know just what rare species he found, because after his death his loyal servants chose to carry back to civilization only those belongings they considered of value, namely his tent, his frying pan and boots, and a few tins of food. Left behind, lost for good, were 'many kinds of flowers and seeds'.

But if Delavay and Farrer were spared knowledge of their losses, the eighteenth-century French botanist and plant hunter Joseph de Jussieu might in retrospect have welcomed such an opportunity. His life is an altogether frightening illustration of the fact that there are worse things than losing one's collections, however painfully acquired. You can also lose your mind.

In 1735 De Jussieu, then a vigorous young botanist of thirty-one, joined a French geographical expedition to Peru commissioned to determine an arc of the meridian. The expedition's target point was high in the Andes, and getting there proved to be agonizingly difficult. De Jussieu, however, who had also trained as a physician, found plenty to interest him in the vast numbers of unfamiliar plant species, especially the mysterious cinchona tree, whose bark was the source of quinine. When, nine years after it began, the expedition members (now much reduced in numbers by disease and accidents) prepared to return home, De Jussieu chose to stay on, partly because of his desire to find more Andean plants, partly because the Spanish colonial government, which required his medical services, wouldn't let him leave.

For another six or eight years, a lonely Frenchman in a strange land, often ill, he worked as a doctor and searched for plants, collecting seeds and living specimens and making notes. He even turned his hand to engineering, building roads and bridges. With difficulty, he succeeded in sending a few new species to his botanist brothers Antoine and Bernard in Paris. But eventually, locking his precious collections and papers in a chest, he headed across the continent to Buenos Aires, intending to accompany them by sea to France.

En route, catastrophe. A trusted servant, convinced that De Jussieu's precious chest in fact contained money, absconded with it over the border into Brazil. Neither the chest nor the servant were ever seen again.

The loss apparently so shocked the good doctor that his wits were affected. Already depressed, he gradually gave up botany and slipped into madness. Not until 1771 did he finally reach Paris, unrecognizable as the man who left for Peru nearly forty years before. By then he had forgotten virtually everything about his real achievements – as the first man to study coca in its native habitat, as the introducer of such valuable plants as the orange ball buddleia (*Buddleja globosa*) and the heliotrope (*Heliotropium arborescens*), as the expert on quinine and the cinchona tree who might have contributed greatly to medical knowledge. For Joseph de Jussieu, loss was complete.

A Slightly Bad Rap

For about 400 years now, John Gerard has borne a severe stain on his character. As the nominal author of *The Herball, or generall historie of plantes*, one of the first major surveys of plants to be published in English and an authentic classic of horticulture, along with his contemporary fame as a gardener, he might have expected better. After all, he was a wonderful writer, capable of expressing himself with all the ease and eloquence of his Elizabethan fellows. Beyond that, he was possessed of wonderful curiosity and patience in gathering botanical facts and (it must be said) apocrypha.

Gerard was born in Cheshire in 1545 and trained as a surgeon, probably as a ship's doctor, becoming eventually a member of the elite Barber-Surgeons' Company in London. As may be guessed from the title of his professional group, practising as a surgeon in the seventeenth century was a rather different matter from what it is today. In addition to removing the odd limb and letting a certain amount of blood, deliberately and otherwise, a surgeon had to deal knowledgeably with *materia medica*, which then consisted largely of plant-based medicines – 'simples'. Being a surgeon consorted closely with being a botanist.

In Gerard's case, it also involved being a gardener. We know that in addition to his doctoring he served for nearly twenty years as superintendent to the gardens of the great Lord Burghley, Queen Elizabeth's chief adviser, in The Strand and at Theobalds, Burghley's Hertfordshire estate. While there is no way of telling just what this duty demanded of him, it must have had something to do with his skill as a horticulturist. George Baker, one of the Queen's own principal doctors, remarked on Gerard's proficiency ('I do not thinke for the knowledge of plants, that he is inferior to any') and described a day spent searching for 'the most rarest simples' with Gerard and a visiting French expert. The result was a clear win for Gerard. 'My French man,' Baker reported, 'did not know one to his fower.'

Of course in that case Gerard was on home ground, which may have given him an advantage. But he was unquestionably a talented plantsman. In 1596, apparently at the urging of admiring friends, he published a complete list of the plants he cultivated in his own London garden. This was in Holborn, probably in the vicinity of what is now Fetter Lane, at that time an upper-class area where he had his house. The list contained upwards of a thousand different species and varieties, many of them unusual. Among other things, he boasted 'thirtie sorts' of plum tree, a plane tree (*Platanus orientalis*) from Greece, martagon lilies (*Lilium chalcedonicum*) from Turkey, yucca from the West Indies, and potatoes (which unfortunately 'perished and rotted' in winter). Most of the plants, as might be expected, were native British specimens, but even here a number were rare – a double-flowered crowfoot found in Lancashire 'by a curious gentleman in the serching foorth of simples,' Venus' looking glass (*Legousia hybrida*) that he 'found in a field among corne by Greenehithe', caltrops (*Tribulus terrestris*) from 'neere Croidon', and a whole range of irises and crocuses.

Perhaps if Gerard had left it at that, resting on his laurels as a better-than-average gardener (and surgeon – in 1608 he would be elected Master of the Barber-Surgeons' Company), he would have saved himself from considerable later calumny. On the other hand, posterity would likely have forgotten him. Instead, in 1597 he published the enormous folio volume that would become famous as *Gerard's Herball*, and seized a place in the annals of botanical history.

The *Herball* is in many ways a delightful book, less for its accuracy than for its enthusiasm and innocence and loving attention to anything that engages the author's interest. The plant descriptions tend to be perfunctory (although some, like that of the crown imperial, are impressively detailed); the real charm of Gerard's text lies in the anecdotal ancillary material – guides to where each of the plants may be found, discussion of the origin of its names, analysis of its 'vertues' as medicine or food.

This last category incidentally says a lot about the state of medical art at the close of the sixteenth century and might, I suppose, even give pause to adherents of alternative medicine at the beginning of the twenty-first. For example, in Gerard's view St John's wort can be used to make a 'a most pretious remedie for deep wounds and those that are thorow the body' (nothing about premenstrual tension). An onion mashed up with salt, rue and honey is supposed to be a specific against the bite of a mad dog. Tobacco is good for all sorts of ailments from bad colds to deafness, although smoking can lead to addiction – some 'cannot forbeare it, no not in the midst of their dinner'. Oddly, since digitalis is one herbal treatment now generally accepted by mainstream medicine (as a heart stimulant), foxgloves (*Digitalis purpurea*) are dismissed as 'of no use, neither have they any place among medicines'.

As a reference work, the *Herball* leaves quite a lot to be desired. Despite its size – later editions grew to 1,600 pages and more than 500,000 words – it is hardly complete. Moreover, many of its medical 'facts' actually date back to such classical authors as Dioscorides, Galen and Pliny. And the pictures are a hodge-podge of woodcuts, some of them mislabelled.

Yet it was a step forward in a long chain of herbals, and given its immediate history its failings can be explained if not necessarily forgiven. The sixteenth century was a time of sweeping interest in botany, as in the other natural sciences; scholars – usually medical men – had produced herbals in France, Germany, Italy, and the Low Countries which were quickly pirated for information and translated into other languages. In England, Gerard had been anticipated by several works, among them William Turner's *Herball* (1551–68) and a translation by Henry Lyte (1578) of a Flemish herbal by Rembert Dodoens. The latter was a typical example of the roundabout way such circulation took place: Lyte actually translated not from Dodoens's original, but from a French translation made by the botanist Charles l'Ecluse (better known as Clusius, and a major figure in science of the time). It was a perfect recipe for confusion.

By the 1590s, it was clear that there was a market for a good new English-language herbal. The London publisher John Norton put together what he thought would be a surefire package: a fresh translation of Dodoens (drawn from his collected works, in Latin, called *Stirpium historiae pemptades sex*) illustrated with the best up-to-date plant pictures. For the translation he hired a London doctor named Robert Priest; for the illustrations he rented the woodblocks used by a Frankfurt publisher in a 1590 German herbal.

Presumably all went well until Priest died, his translation incomplete. It is impossible to judge how much there was left to do when Norton went to his Holborn neighbour John Gerard and suggested that he take over. In any event, Gerard apparently jumped at the opportunity, and set about elaborating the basic text with homely anecdotes, personal comments on medical matters and many reports on locations where particular plants could be found. His own circle of botanical connections ranged from Sir Walter Raleigh to a ship's doctor; they supplied him with both plants and information, much of which he incorporated. He also offered horticultural notes, for example telling how he lost his hibiscus (*Hibiscus sabdariffa*) in a hard frost and boasting of his success with beetroots.

Somehow or other, Gerard began to feel possessive about the project, perhaps excessively so. His introduction makes the matter uncomfortably obvious. In it he flatly states that poor Priest had perished, unable to finish the work, and 'his translation likewise perished'. The obvious implication is that Gerard had done it all himself; he speaks of 'these mine own labours'. In her history of herbals, the botanist Agnes Arber calls this 'a deliberate lie', and supports her opinion by pointing out that Gerard's claim is contradicted a comment in a prefatory letter by another writer actually printed at the front of the *Herball*.

Nor was being named as a plagiarist his only problem. Admittedly lacking in scientific sophistication – he calls himself 'but a Countrey Schollar' – Gerard had managed to get a number of pictures attached to the wrong plant description. When the publisher engaged a rival expert, Mathias de l'Obel (namesake of the lobelia, and a Frenchman then resident in England) to straighten them out, Gerard bridled. Claiming that L'Obel's English wasn't up to the job, he forced him to give up making corrections before he was finished, and the book went to press as was.

Gerard might have done better to stay home in Holborn with his caltrops. Although his *Herball* quickly became a publishing success, more criticism lay in wait. The volume concludes with a section on what the author calls 'one of the marvels of this land (we may say of the World)': 'The Goose tree, Barnacle tree, or the tree bearing Geese'. A marvel indeed – a tree that produces live geese! Such unlikely plants were said to be found in northern Scotland and the Orkneys, and although Gerard was not prepared to swear to their existence, he was happy to vouch for something nearly as good. 'What our eies have seen, and hands have touched we shall declare,' he declares, before launching into an account of finding, on a small island off Lancashire, certain mussel-shaped shells containing tiny infant birds that matured into tree geese. You could buy 'one of the best' fully grown for threepence.

The most effective (if subversive) attack on Gerard came a quarter of a century after his death in 1612, when Thomas Johnson, a London apothecary, botanist, and plant hunter, undertook a revision and updating of the *Herball*. Johnson pulled no punches. He found plenty to correct, and made a point of emphasizing that they *were* corrections. Thus under Gerard's note on location for 'Alkanet or wilde Buglosse', Johnson remarks sourly: 'I doubt whether our Author found any of these in the place here set down, for I have sought it but failed of finding.'

Gerard had made claims of native British origin for a number of plants. These particularly annoyed Johnson, who plainly knew more about the subject than his predecessor. One such claim in particular roused the editor's ire, and has been held against Gerard ever since. 'The male Pieonie,' he had stated, 'groweth wild upon a conny berry [rabbit warren] in Betsome . . . in Kent.' In his note on the passage, Johnson wrote: 'I have been told that our Author himselfe planted that Peionie there, and afterwards seems to finde it there by accident; and I doe beleeve it was so, because none before or since have ever seene or heard of it growing wilde in any part of this kingdome.' Whump. With that, in addition to plagiarism, inaccuracy and credulous ignorance, Gerard – who was of course no longer on the scene to defend himself – stood indicted on charges of corruption.

While I'm in no position to answer these charges in any detail – is anyone? – it does seem to me that posterity has been at least slightly unfair to John Gerard. Does his book actually deserve to be called, in the words of one modern historian, 'the production of a rogue'? Possibly he did make more use of the deceased Dr Priest's translation than he had a right to, but I'm ready to forgive a lot to anyone who could describe a ripe dandelion head as 'a round downy blowbal', or call botanizing 'a study for the wisest, an exercise for the noblest, a pastime for the best', or name a wild clematis 'travellers' joy' (the name stuck).

Was he too credulous? Well, he bought the tree geese, but so did plenty of others at the time (along with the Vegetable Lamb – see pages 102–6); circumstantial accounts of the phenomenon were still being published at the end of the eighteenth century, according to a bizarre little study by Edward Heron-Allen entitled *Barnacles in Nature and Myth*. Moreover, if he is to be attacked for gullibility, he ought to be given credit for his splendid demolition job on the hoary (and widely accepted) legend of the mandrake ('there hath beene many ridiculous tales brought up of this plant'), whose root doesn't in fact have a human shape or 'give a great shreeke' when it is pulled up.

As for Gerard's discovery of a peony growing wild in Kent, stranger things have happened. It might have been better if he hadn't planted it first, but even here he is not alone. In the 1940s, a prominent professor of botany named John Heslop Harrison announced that he had found several rare plants, hitherto unknown in Britain, on the Hebridean island of Rum. It was years before a suspicious Cambridge classicist and amateur botanist established beyond any doubt that Heslop Harrison had in fact faked the discoveries with a bit of sleight-of-hand trowel-work. In Gerard's case, we have only the word of a notably hostile editor.

Yet if Thomas Johnson was less than kind to John Gerard personally, he did do him a great favour in revising the *Herball* with such skill. The 1633 edition – and a further edition in 1636 – became the standard text for botanists both professional and amateur over more than a century. In another sense it is still exceptionally valuable. An American rare book dealer recently advertised a copy of Gerard's first edition for no less than $13,850.

Nutmeg, Clove and
Peter Pepper

It may say something about my lightness of mind, but my curiosity can be aroused by a name alone. That was true of the Tradescants, of Philibert Commerson, and certainly of Englebert Kaempfer. In each case, further investigation turned out to be highly satisfying to anyone with a taste like mine for the extraordinary. These were amazing people, who did amazing things in the field of botany and plant-hunting and gardening.

It was for much the same reason that I decided to explore the doings of another man whose name struck me as suitably odd. Pierre Poivre – *anglice* Peter Pepper – appeared to have played a central role in the botany and the business of the spice trade in the eighteenth century. Improbably enough, however, I found that his name had absolutely nothing to do with his achievements. What he cared about were cloves and nutmeg, not pepper. But he cared about them with a passion. That the world today has all the cloves and nutmeg is needs or wants is largely his doing – to say nothing of the hundreds of exotic plants he was responsible for bringing into our gardens.

Pierre Poivre (Le Poivre in his grander days) was born in Lyons in 1719, the son of a merchant of ribbon and braid. An intelligent and active boy, a painter and a good Latin scholar, he took a particular interest in plants. By 1740 he was at the Missions

Étrangères in Paris pursuing studies for the priesthood, but there is some reason to doubt that he saw the Church as his future. Foreign travel, on the other hand, was worth a mass, and while still a student he wangled a trip to China with a group of missionaries. He was already extremely knowledgeable in botany.

Poivre spent four years in Canton and Cochin-China, as the southern part of Vietnam was then known. His activities were not very religious; in fact within a short time of his arrival he was in prison, denounced by the authorities as a dangerous person. As a favour to a friend he had attempted to deliver a seditious letter written in Chinese – which he didn't understand. Undaunted by incarceration, he set out to learn Chinese in order to conduct his own defence, and so impressed the local viceroy that he was pardoned. More than that: the viceroy gave him unprecedented permission to travel inland along the Hsi Chiang river up to the foothills of the Nan Ling range, where he botanized and made notes on everything from silkworms to star anise.

In 1745, Poivre made up his mind to return to France, possibly to take orders as a priest. Packing his notebooks and his boxes of specimens, he set sail on a well-armed French vessel for the long journey back. Off Sumatra, nemesis in the form of a British man-of-war hove into sight and in the ensuing battle Poivre (whose priestly demeanour left something to be desired anyway) joined in vigorously and lost his right hand. He also lost all his collections and, briefly, his freedom, before the British put him ashore at the Dutch East Indies capital of Batavia to recuperate.

As he later put it in his memoirs, the amputation meant that he could no longer hope to be priest, because he could not consecrate the host. But he now fortuitously found himself in a position to pursue quite another career.

The Dutch East India Company possessed an absolute monopoly on the production and sale of cloves and nutmeg.

Through brutal expropriations, bribery and diplomacy, as well as tight restrictions on the export of seeds and plants, the company maintained firm control of the market. And it was an incredibly profitable market: in 1670, thanks mainly to the spice trade in the Moluccas, the company was the richest corporation in the world, paying its shareholders an annual dividend of 40 per cent.

During the five months he spent in Batavia, working as a tutor and learning to write with his left hand, Poivre discovered a great deal about the spice business in the Dutch East Indies. It was jealously protected. Both clove trees (*Syzygium aromaticum*) and nutmeg trees (*Myristica fragrans*) had been native species originally widely scattered across the vast archipelago now known as Indonesia, but in the interest of controlling production the Dutch had concentrated the plantations in two tiny areas in the Moluccas – the island of Amboina in the case of cloves, and for nutmegs three small islands in the Banda Group. All were heavily guarded.

As a botanist, Poivre recognized that the spice trees depended on a moist equatorial climate to thrive. Such climates existed elsewhere, however, for example on Isle de France in the Indian Ocean (since 1810 known as Mauritius), which had been a port of call on his journey from France. If it was possible to secure some plants or fertile seeds, he believed, the Dutch monopoly would be broken. This could not be accomplished straightforwardly, of course, but it was said that within the Moluccas – a scattering of some fifty large and small islands – there were other places where spice trees might be found. He decided to go back to France and present a plan to the royal authorities.

Calamity at sea seems to have pursued Pierre Poivre and this trip was no exception. He got as far as the coast of Siam in a French brigatine called the *Favori* before it sank in high seas; boarding another vessel, he managed to get to India, in some disorder from sickness and pain in his arm; and finally reached Mauritius, where he immediately reembarked for Europe, his luggage stuffed with seeds of rare plants. This time pirates seized the vessel as it was entering the English Channel, and a few days after they had boarded it an English frigate loomed out of the fog and attacked. All the French passengers, including Poivre, were thrown in chains and imprisoned in Guernsey. Not until a year later, with the signing of a peace treaty between England and France, was he able to return to his homeland.

At thirty, he was no longer an unknown student. Fluent in Chinese, Malay and Vietnamese, able to speak with authority on eastern countries and their plants, possessing first-hand information about trade – and especially the Dutch monopolies – Poivre was a man to be heard. With France at the height of its power, the French East India Company was eager to expand. It met his ideas with ready acceptance. These included establishing warehouses and trade centres in Indochina with connections to India, the Cape and the East Indies and – most important – transplanting the precious spice trees to Mauritius and nearby Isle-de-Bourbon (Réunion). His intention was to turn these French possessions into enormously profitable tropical farms. And, he confided to such important French botanists and natural historians as George-Louis Leclerc Buffon and Louis Guillaume Lemonnier, he would also create a private garden to raise rare plants, where newly discovered species could be acclimatized and – if suitable for cultivation in Europe – prepared for safe shipment. He would be able to supply complete information on soil and water requirements, flowering time and so forth.

His scheme approved, Poivre once again headed east, and this time reached Cochin-China unharmed. He was immediately plunged into a morass of frustrating diplomacy which delayed his planned journey onwards to Manila where, he had been told, he would be able to pick up specimens of both nutmeg and clove plants from smugglers. In the meantime, he took the opportunity to send cinnamon and pepper trees, along with dye, resin and varnish plants, from Southeast Asia to Mauritius. He also found a kind of rice that would grow on dry land.

In the event, it was more than two years before he reached the Philippines, only to find that competitors were already at work. But Poivre was ingenious and knew more about plants than his rivals. He managed to get a quantity of fertile nutmegs from a Chinese merchant (the Dutch normally treated the nuts with lime before shipment, so they wouldn't germinate) and raised thirty-odd healthy seedlings. Sending word back to Mauritius that a garden should be prepared to receive the plants, he also asked the governor for a ship in which he could venture to the Moluccas himself in search of cloves. In the Philippines, he had drawn a blank; the cloves of commerce were buds, not seeds, and there was no hope of raising seedlings from them.

Poivre was getting desperate. The governor's ship never arrived. Two Spanish vessels commissioned to reach the Spice Islands failed to sail. A trip back to the French colony of Pondicherry on the south-east coast of India to plead for help came to nothing. He finally returned to Mauritius, shipping his precious nutmeg plants separately – only five arrived there alive – and managed to talk the governor into letting him use an aged and decrepit 100-ton frigate for yet another journey east. This time he would turn pirate himself.

Poivre later wrote a hair-raising account of his trip in *La Colombe*. The ship was so old and badly built that it wouldn't sail to windward; when it approached the island of Meyo, where cloves were reportedly abundant, it was unable to land. Poivre finally fetched up in Portuguese Timor, where he paid an intermediary 14,000 piastres for twenty clove and twenty nutmeg plants; when they were never delivered he undertook a raid and seized some specimens on his own. On the way back to Mauritius, the French ship narrowly escaped being taken by a Dutch patrol; Poivre ingeniously ran up a Dutch flag at the last minute.

His homecoming to Mauritius in 1755 should have been triumphant. After all, he had introduced both nutmegs and cloves. But disaster awaited him. The nutmeg plants he had shipped from the Philippines were all dead, in spite of his detailed instructions for their care and cultivation. What's worse, the Company's botanist and apothecary, an obviously jealous gentleman named Fusée Aublet, officially declared that the clove and nutmeg plants brought from Timor with such difficulty were fakes. Placed in the care of M. Fusée Aublet, they predictably expired.

In a sense, Pierre Poivre was a failure. In other ways he was anything but. During his struggles to secure cloves and nutmegs, he had succeeded in sending back to his botanist friends in France an impressive range of other plants, among them double-flowered lilies, the citron tree (*Citrus medica*), various hydrangeas, balsam, scented acacias, irises, an amaranthus, the wild nutmeg *Monodora myristica*, cinnamon and cassia (*Cinnamomum zylanicum* and *C. cassia*) and the Madagascar clove (*Ravensara aromatica*), which he had hopes of developing as a spice plant. One vetch, *Hedysarum lutescens*, has never been found again. In all, he could boast the discovery of more than 800 hitherto unknown species. In Mauritius, moreover, he was largely responsible for the establishment of what would become one of the great botanic gardens of the world. The Jardin de Pamplemousses (literally Grapefruit Garden – the name actually comes from its location in the Pamplemousses district a few miles from the Mauritian capital, Port Louis) had existed in a vague way before Poivre's time, but it was his efforts that began filling it with plants from all round the Southern Oceans, from Africa to Indonesia.

With the appointment of a governor unsympathetic to his plans, Poivre decided to retire to France. Yet again, on the journey home, he was captured by the English, but spent only a short time interned in Cork and was soon comfortably settled in a small estate near Lyons. He wrote, joined scholarly societies and continued to tell anyone who would listen that the only hope for Mauritius – whose economy had fallen into such disarray that the Company finally gave up and ceded it to the Crown – was the spice trade. Ten years passed. Suddenly, the call came: Mauritius would have a new governor, and Poivre would be given the important post of Commissaire-Ordonnateur et Intendant Général, with the primary task of establishing the cultivation of clove and nutmeg trees.

It was the only offer that could have tempted him from his comfortable existence in the Lyonnais. By 1767 he was once again in Mauritius with his new wife, busily developing the Jardin de Pamplemousses and plotting – now with real hope of success – how to lay hands on the priceless spice trees.

It is clear from surviving documents that Poivre never had clear sailing as an administrator in Mauritius. He was constantly at odds with a series of governors who regarded him as an impractical enthusiast, fixated on his plants, while conditions desperately needing attention got none. Port Louis itself was an unpleasant place; Poivre himself described it as 'a moral and physical sewer', where one was 'equally in danger of assassination, plague or fire'. But this time, with considerable authority in his own hands, he could organize and finance expeditions in quest of spice trees.

In 1770, the payoff finally arrived. Poivre had secretly sent two corvettes commanded by young officers to the Moluccas. After months of searching (including a narrow escape from death in an earthquake and gun battles with hostile locals), they fortunately fell in with a renegade Dutchman who told them they could find clove saplings and seed nutmegs on a small island called Guéby. The sultan of Guéby, moreover, was friendly. The expedition was consequently able to deliver a magnificent haul to the eagerly waiting Poivre in Port Louis: 450 nutmeg saplings, 70 clove trees 'with their leaves very green, and very aromatic'; 10 germinating clove seeds; 100 more seeds in a separate case, plus many clove plants that suffered during the passage 'but still gave hope'; 5 cases containing about 10,000 nutmegs, 'mostly germinating'; and another case of nutmegs beginning to root. On hand to confirm the authenticity of the species was none other than the royal naturalist Philibert Commerson (see page 89), with whom even the egregious Fusée Aublet could not argue. The Dutch monopoly was effectively broken at last.

In 1773, for the last time, Poivre returned to France, where he died in 1786. He left behind the thriving Jardin de Pamplemousses (having been sold to the king, it was now a royal garden) with a host of new plants, many of which were sent on to Europe – nasturtiums, a storksbill geranium, gladioli, white rocket, seven types of aloe, tuberoses, mignonettes. The first cloves would be harvested on Mauritius in 1777, and nutmegs the next year.

But the cultivation of the spices had proved to be less certain than hoped. Within a year of their arrival only fifty nutmeg and fourteen clove plants were left alive. A second equally chancy expedition to the Moluccas supplemented their number. During Poivre's last days in the colony he so plagued his successor as Intendant with advice on caring for his plants that the new man complained he had no time left for administrative duties. The real weight of responsibility for them, however, fell on the shoulders of the horticulturist Poivre had chosen to run the royal garden, Jean-Nicolas de Céré, a skilled plantsman. Gradually, Céré coaxed a fair number into maturity.

The nutmegs posed an unsuspected problem. Céré discovered that they were unisexual. Only the female plants bore fruit. This made multiplying them extremely difficult, since the sex could not be determined by available methods, and male plants outnumbered female by five to one. Quite apart from such technical considerations, cultivation of the trees required a great deal more patience, attention and hard work than most of the Mauritian colonists were inclined to devote to them. Céré cynically suspected that most of the seed nutmegs he distributed ended up in planters' kitchens.

Poivre worried that the soil and weather in Mauritius was not, after all, suitable for the precious trees. There was also the dire possibility that a hurricane or other natural disaster could wipe out the entire lot. Against some opposition, before leaving for France he sent specimens to other French tropical colonies – to Réunion, Cayenne, and the Seychelles. It was not long before plants began slipping out to other regions, to Madagascar and Zanzibar, to South America and West Africa. The French tried to keep control, but with only modest success. Céré did his best. On one occasion in 1789 a group of ambassadors from the important Indian ruler Tippoo Sahib flatly refused to leave Mauritius without spice plants. The island, virtually bankrupt because of the French Revolution, could not afford to entertain the envoys any longer; so Céré was ordered to deliver the goods. His clever solution: he supplied two male nutmegs, and secured a promise from the captain of the ambassadors' ship to drown the clove plants in boiling water *en route*.

Ironically, despite all the efforts of Pierre Poivre, Céré and the rest, neither cloves nor nutmegs brought wealth to Mauritius (sugarcane is the main crop). Today cloves are grown all through the tropics, with Brazil and Madagascar the main producers. About half end up, literally, in smoke, in the clove cigarettes Indonesians favour. Nutmeg (and mace, the lacy outer covering of the nuts) continues to come mainly from Indonesia and, more recently, from Grenada in the West Indies. The Jardin de Pamplemousses, having had considerable ups and down since the eighteenth century, now bears the resounding name of Sir Seewoosagur Ramgoolam Botanical Garden, after the founding father of modern Mauritius. It still contains a staggering variety of tropical plants – including eighty-five varieties of palms, giant water lilies and lotuses, lichees, breadfruit and, naturally, nutmegs and cloves.

Sir Walter's Trees

I am a fan of Sir Walter Scott. Not so much of the novels –
though some of those are pretty good too – but of Scott the man,
the history-mad Borderer, the collector of ballads, the
bibliophile, the dreamer on great houses who actually built one,
the naïve businessman willing to write himself into the grave in
order to pay off debts that he might well have disclaimed. A
heroic figure, in short, yet one whose ordinary humanity
emerged irrepressibly over and over again throughout his life –
and perhaps never more so than in his fascination with gardening.

Technically, I suppose, we shouldn't speak of his 'gardening'.
He would not have approved. He was a tree man, a planter. All
his life he had loved trees, and when he undertook to create
Abbotsford, the country estate he built beside the Tweed near
Melrose, it was clothing the barren hills that he saw as his first
goal. Again and again, in his letters and journal and his
miscellaneous writings, he speaks of this ambition. 'Where no
one else can see anything but fallow and broom and furze, I am
anticipating lawns and groves,' he wrote in 1812, soon after
purchasing the first 120-acre section of the property. 'I have got
nature in a very naked state to work upon.' Abbotsford would
grow, before his death in 1832, to nearly 1,500 acres – of which
more than a third were indeed covered by 'groves'.

His arboreal obsession was longstanding. The most memorable feature of a garden he had known as a boy was an enormous plane tree – 'a huge hill of leaves' – under which he enjoyed sitting to read. He movingly describes looking for it years later, only to find the tree dead and the garden wrecked. 'We were glad when we could leave it.' Another retrospective excursion, described by his son-in-law and biographer John Gibson Lockhart, was happier. Searching for the small cottage which had been his first country home when newly married ten years earlier, he found that the 'two miserable willow trees' he had tied together to form an arch over the gate had matured into a handsome ivy-clad bower.

No sooner had Scott purchased Abbotsford than he began planting, 'throwing my money, not indeed upon the waters, but upon the earth, in hopes of seeing it, after many days, in the shape of shrubs and trees'. Friends sent him fruit trees, which he carefully planted; other friends, at his request, came through with 'cartloads' of acorns that he fondly hoped would sprout and 'make a great show'. Some did, modestly – 'the future oaks [are] nearly as tall as your knitting needle,' he boasted in a thank-you note, and the next year 'some of my newly planted trees actually rival an expanded umbrella in height and extent of shade'. But on the whole the acorns were a flop. 'Only tens,' he mused, 'were left out of hundreds and thousands. The mice had probably their share in bringing about this catastrophe; the hares still a greater one.' In combination with another fiasco – a shipment of Portuguese chestnuts intended for sowing arrived peeled and boiled – he arrived at the conclusion that 'planting seeds in wild country is a very doubtful measure'. The best solution was saplings from 'a well-managed nursery'.

He had to learn on the job. 'I am not a little puzzled,' he admitted, 'in my attempts to acquire some knowledge of shrubs and trees. . . . I asked a lady the other day what shrub it was that had a leaf like a saddle, and was much edified by learning that it was the tulip tree. By such awkward steps do learners ascend the ladder of knowledge.' But in spite of his inexperience the planting went on apace – shrubs like holly, privet, sweetbrier, honeysuckle, wild roses, white convolvulus ('which would thrive beautifully with blackthorn') on banks and in hedges, trees such as spruce, maritime pine, silver fir, alder, willow, poplar and (mainly) oak. He bewailed the difficulty of getting birch seed, given the ubiquity of birch in the Scottish wild.

Just how the new forests would be spread across the bleak hills of Selkirkshire was a matter of deep concern. 'I am torturing my brains for the best means of conquering the prim regularity of artificial plantations,' he complained. What he wanted were trees 'mingling as if by chance'. In this, as in his other opinions about landscape design, Scott showed himself to be an up-to-date connoisseur of the latest thinking in garden design.

For this was the era of the Picturesque. By the end of the eighteenth century writers like Uvedale Price and Richard Payne Knight had offered a convincing – and on the whole successful – challenge to the long reign of 'Capability' Brown. Where Brown had demanded sweeping manicured lawns, elegant sinuous lakes, and clumps of trees strategically scattered across the landscape, Knight and Price called for wildness and irregularity, intricacy, unpredictability and romance, for a style, in short, that reflected the beauties found in the paintings of such masters as Claude and Salvator Rosa. It is easy for anyone who has read Scott's romantic novels to see why he would have sympathized with this approach. That he did so is obvious not only from his work at Abbotsford but from two long and fascinating essays that he wrote on the subject of planting and landscape design.

The first, which appeared in the *Quarterly Review* in 1824, bore the title 'On Planting Waste Lands'. Based, he says, on 'sixteen years of undeviating attention to the raising of young plantations of considerable extent', it spelled out in practical detail not only why tree-planting made good economic sense, but how it could be employed to enhance the beauty of the landscape. Not, of course, that it was always so employed: he vigorously attacked the practice of planting in straight lines and in patches on hillsides that are likely to remind the observer 'of pincushions, of penny tarts, of breeches displayed at an old-clothesman's door'. Most important was a sensitive respect for the shape of the land to be planted, and an equally sensitive choice of trees. I was pleased to note, incidentally, his lack of enthusiasm for the larch, which I share; while he admits its value as timber, he deplores its 'poverty of aspect' and its excessive formality. Formality, after all, is to Scott the primary sin. As a step toward combatting it he is perfectly happy to let such 'volunteers' as holly, bird-cherries, rowans and various thorns spring up among his trees – they merely serve 'to beautify the operations of art'. (If need be, he was prepared to help out by introducing 'a few wild roses, honeysuckles and sweetbriers . . . to produce the luxuriance we see in the woods which Nature plants herself.')

'On Planting Waste Lands' was actually billed as a book review; his other horticultural essay, 'On Landscape Gardening' (1828), similarly began as a review, of a book by an eccentric Scottish gentleman named Sir Henry Steuart. Steuart had made a name for himself developing techniques for transplanting large trees. Scott regarded him as something of a joke ('Oh Lord, what a fantastical ape he is') but had evident respect for his tree-moving tactics. Much of the essay is devoted to a description of these. The first section, however, deals more generally with Scott's ideas on gardening, and the basis of his opposition to 'Capability' Brown and 'the school of spade and mattock'.

As he sees it, garden historians like Horace Walpole failed to make the important distinction between 'garden' and 'park'. Walpole praised Brown's predecessor William Kent as the man who 'leaped the fence and saw that all nature was a garden'. What Kent – and Walpole – failed to recognize, however, was that the garden itself – the 'pleasance', the walled, flower-filled quarter associated with the house – was a very different thing from the 'park' outside. The garden was, and should be, nothing less than an 'extension of the splendour of the residence into a certain limited portion of the domain'. A good garden thus represents 'the triumph of human art over the elements'. Consequently, in Scott's famous phrase, 'nothing is more completely the child of art than a garden'. A park, on the other hand, is meant to be extensive and wild, anything but artificial.

What this confusion meant in the hands of Kent (whom Scott regarded as 'tame and cold of spirit' with no knowledge of 'the grander scenes of nature'), was the exile of garden either to 'some distant corner' – or oblivion. The bare park came up to the house. The theory had been was to lend the park some of the refinement of the garden, but in the event – and especially under Brown – the landscaping simply became bland and over-calculated, 'not simplicity but affectation labouring to seem simple'. Only with Knight and Price had matters started to improve, as gardens once more began making an appearance near the house and a more sophisticated and natural form of landscape design came into fashion. Such landscape design was, by the way, a business for real artists, including gentlemen of taste. Mere gardening, on the other hand – and here Scott showed his colours – could be handled by skilled labourers.

No doubt that was the case with the garden at Abbotsford. Apart from reporting its original creation ('I have got a good wall built around a sheltered and fertile spot of about ½ of an acre, which I hope will make a clever little garden') he scarcely mentions it in personal terms, although he occasionally notes the activity of his gardener. The fact is that, compared with trees, Scott seems to have rather mistrusted flowers. Possibly the Border winds and fogs played a part in this. 'It is as imprudent to attach yourself to flowers in Scotland as to a caged bird,' he once remarked. 'The cat sooner or later snaps one up.' But he was ready to enjoy plants capable of looking out for themselves. When the time came to tear down the jasmine- and rose-covered porch of the original cottage at Abbotsford so that the foundations of the new building could be laid, he could not bear to kill off the mature climbers. Waiting until winter, he painstakingly dug up as many as he could and transplanted them at his daughter's house of Chiefswood not far away.

Sir Walter Scott might find it ironic that Abbotsford is today celebrated largely for its gardens, while his beloved trees have grown into forests and been felled. Great lawns, topiary, herbaceous borders flaming with summer blossoms – beautiful and striking they may be, but perhaps not exactly what would have been expected by the man who said 'Trees remain the most proper and most manageable material of picturesque improvement' – and never stopped planting.

Getting it Wrong with Sir Francis Bacon

There may be some strange logic in the fact that if you look up Francis Bacon in the stacks of the London Library, what you find is an indiscriminate mixture of books on Sir Francis Bacon (1561–1626), first Baron Verulam and Viscount St Albans, Lord Chancellor and all-round philospher/lawyer/scientist, and Francis Bacon (1909–92), brilliant Fitzrovian painter and wide boy. They have extraordinarily little to do with each other. Yet the confusion might have amused Sir Francis, whose interests were broader, and deeper, than nearly anybody of his time. No doubt he would have had plenty to say about painting, had anyone asked. Almost everything else under the sun fell beneath his gaze at one time or another, including gardening.

Bacon's short essay 'Of Gardens', with its familiar opening ('God Almighty first planted a garden; and indeed it is the purest of human pleasures.'), makes splendidly clear how gardening delighted him. It must have been a refreshing change from his difficult and sometimes dangerous involvement with politics, to say nothing of his ambition to supplant Aristotle as a thinker. How he found the time can only be conjectured. His approach to horticulture, moreover, was anything but theoretical. Beneath its Elizabethan exuberance of language, 'Of Gardens' is nothing more or less than a practical guide for a nobleman in need of a garden. Provided you had a minimum of 30 acres to spare, Bacon offers instruction on layout, on associated buildings and – most of all – on exactly what to plant in the various portions of your demesne for colour, perfume or fruit. His ideal, like that of such other seventeenth century gardeners as John Evelyn, was *ver perpetuum* – perpetual green or 'gardens for all the months in the year'.

Not a great deal is known about Bacon's own activities as a gardener. In the 1590s he is said to have set out lime and birch saplings at Twickenham Park in the form of a maze, and his plantings at the Inns of Court in the same period were apparently extensive – some 40,000 privet and quickset shrubs forming hedges, plus willows, rose standards, honeysuckle and other climbers. No doubt he embellished his mansion at Gorhambury near St Albans in the best fashion of the time.

His essay 'Of Gardens' is full of praise for individual species – pinks and gillyflowers (stocks), honeysuckles, mezereon (*Daphne mezereum*), 'the early tulippa'. That Bacon knew the plants personally is obvious, and not just as a rich man with a staff of gardeners, either. To get a real sense of how intimate his dealings with plants could be, however, we must look at another, less likely source.

When he died in 1626 (of a bad cold caught, typically enough, during an experimental attempt to preserve the flesh of a chicken by stuffing the carcass with snow), Bacon was in the process of compiling a huge, vastly miscellaneous collection of facts, theories, hypotheses and proposed experiments about all kinds of natural phenomena from drunkenness to the conversion of base metals to gold. The collection had a point: it was meant to be the underpinning for a practical new philosophical approach. Bacon aimed to uncover the secrets of nature by organized observation, which involved the accumulation of data, judicious interpretation and experimentation to establish the accuracy of the material brought together. Given that it was then still thought possible to grasp all of human knowledge in one go, Bacon's compendium was bound to be enormous.

Of course he never had a chance to finish it. In its published form, apparently arranged for the press just after his death by his chaplain, William Rawley, *Sylva Sylvarum* (which means something in the order of 'The Ultimate Forest', referring to 'the forest of experience') consists of ten 'centuries' of one hundred items each – only a fraction, one may assume, of the never-completed whole. Luckily for us, two of the centuries and a part of a third are devoted to horticultural matters – advice, first- and second-hand observations, experiments, theories. It is invariably fascinating, and I'd like to be able to say that Bacon's fellow gardeners today would find it useful. In fact, however, by modern standards these sections of *Sylva Sylvarum* are full of bizarre errors and botanical improbabilities. Bacon is not always wrong, but you wouldn't want to follow his footsteps too closely.

For example, there is his conviction that failure to cultivate a plant with due care and attention may actually make it degenerate into a form that is 'baser in the same kind; sometimes so far as to change into another kind'. Colewort (brassica such as kale) might turn into rape, or 'water-mint into field-mint'. Very old seeds, provided they still have the strength to germinate, are likely to produce a degenerate plant. Drought can cause degeneration, as can transplanting into poorer soil. Exposing basil to excessive sun (impossible in England, in my experience) may make it decline into thyme. Neglect could even cause coloured flowers to turn white. Then there was transmutation. Bacon reports an 'old tradition, that boughs of oak put into the earth will put forth wild vines'. He goes on to doubt whether it is the oak that is changing into the vine, however, theorizing that the earth may be producing the vine spontaneously after being 'qualified' by the decay of the oak.

Bacon's doubts about the oak boughs is typical; he frequently displays a modern scepticism about more outlandish received beliefs while at the same time coming up with explanations no less unlikely. Mulberries, he has heard, 'will be fairer, and the tree more fruitful' if you bore holes in the trunk and hammer in wedges of wood from 'some hot trees, as turpentine [pine], mastic-tree [*Pistacia lentiscus*], guaiacum, juniper &c'. The reason it works, he concludes, is that 'adventive heat doth cheer up the native juice of the tree'. No mention of the obvious discomfort caused the poor mulberry.

Fruit trees come in for a lot of attention, some of it constructive. In the latter category is Bacon's advice to loosen the soil around the roots each year, cultivating and renewing with new earth and compost. Possibly less plausible is his proposal that piling a heap of flint or other stone around the trunk will make the tree 'prosper double', or that nursery trees shouldn't be pampered with rich ground, because 'hardness in youth lengtheneth life . . . it is good to begin with the hardest, as dancing in thick shoes &c'. And if a tree won't bear, there's nothing for it but to bore a hole into its heart to let some of the excess sap out. Otherwise, a salutary process is 'hacking trees in their bark, both downright and across'. This keeps them for being 'hidebound'.

As Bacon would have been the first to admit, there's much more to gardening than being strict with your fruit trees. In one particularly interesting passage, he discusses – and partly debunks – what we know today as companion planting, or 'sympathy and antipathy of plants'. The notion of plants showing any 'secret friendship or hatred', he argues, is an 'idle and ignorant conceit'. Yet some plants do grow better in particular company – rue, for instance, 'doth prosper much . . . if it be set by a fig tree,' while 'certain corn-flowers' such as 'blue-bottle [*Centaurea cyanus*], a kind of yellow marygold, wild poppy, and fumitory' grow 'only amongst corn'. The explanation, according to Bacon, is that different plants require different 'juices' from the soil, and when both need the same juice, both suffer. Conversely, when they demand 'contrary' juices, they will thrive, and especially so when one species 'qualifies' the earth for the other, as corn seems to do for the cornflowers.

Given the state of knowledge of plant nutriments at the beginning of the sevententh century, Bacon's reasoning is sound enough, and certainly an improvement over vegetable love and hatred. He goes on, moreover, to speculate about a related phenomenon, the belief that companion planting can improve the quality of a given crop. The 'ancients', he says, thought that planting rue and figs together not only made the rue stronger, but also made the figs sweeter. Likewise, planting garlic next to roses was supposed to make the roses more fragrant, presumably because 'the more fetid juices of the earth goeth into the garlic, and the more odorate into the rose'.

At this point, however, Bacon's characteristic eagerness to test facts kicks in, and he proposes a series of experiments aimed at proving his theory of 'juices'. 'Take wormwood, or rue, and set it near lettuce, or coleflory [cauliflower], or artichoke, and see whether the lettuce, or the coleflory, &c., become not the sweeter.' Do the same with cucumbers and muskmelons, sorrel and raspberries, a service-tree and a grapevine. See whether a 'common brier' planted with violets or wallflowers will not make them 'sweeter, and less earthy in their smell'. He doesn't seem to have tried these experiments himself – Bacon was a very busy man – but apparently thought they would work. Even so, of course, results might be modest. You shouldn't, he cautions, expect 'a gross difference by this culture, but only farther perfection'.

Sylva Sylvarum proposes many other experiments, some dealing with ways to make plants flower or bear earlier, others with techniques for improving cultivars by grafting and the like. Bacon is adamant, in spite of contemporary arguments to the contrary, that in grafting the scion is always dominant over the stock; other theories are 'imaginations, and untrue'. In other words, there is no way to make a late-bearing scion bear earlier by grafting it on to an early-bearing stock. In this, of course, he is dead right. The gardener or nurseryman intent on crossbreeding must rely on other tactics.

If indeed there were any. 'The compounding or mixture of plants is not found out,' Bacon remarks regretfully. 'It were one of the most noble experiments touching plants to find it out; for you may have great variety of new fruits and flowers yet unknown.' The mystery remained to be solved since various attempts to do so had been, in his eyes, only marginally successful. One involved binding flattened twigs tightly together and planting them; they might 'put forth their several fruits' although there would be 'no commixture in the fruit'. But he heard of setting tightly bound red and white grapevines together to produce 'grapes of several colours upon the same branch; and grape-stones of several colours within the same grape'. In this case, after a year or two, 'the unity' grew 'more perfect'. He also had hopes of another method – wrapping 'divers seeds' in a cloth and planting them 'in earth well-dunged', whereupon the 'shoots would incorporate'. But was it likely? 'The unity of continuance is easier to procure than the unity of species,' Bacon commented ruefully, a man as usual well ahead of his time. It would be a couple of centuries before Gregor Mendel got a real grip on the 'compounding or mixture of plants'.

Even in its fragmentary state (Bishop Tenison, writing in the 1670s, described *Sylva Sylvarum* as 'thrown together in a heap . . . the most extraordinary jumble of facts and observation that has ever been brought together . . . a high kind of natural magic'), Bacon's great compendium is impossible to comprehend in detail. Would you have guessed that root crops such as carrots and parsnips are 'more sweet and luscious' in plague years, presumably because of 'putrefaction' in the soil and air? That when it comes to nourishing a plant, water is 'almost all in all', and earth does no more than keep the plant upright and save it from 'over-heat and over-cold'? That white flowers are always relatively odourless?

In 1658, an expert horticulturist named Ralph Austen, himself author of books on grafting and gardening, published a pamphlet attacking (in a gentlemanly fashion) a number of Bacon's statements. As for white flowers lacking in scent, for example, Austen harrumphs 'I conceive this experiment was not thoroughly weighed.' On cutting or boring fruit trees – such a practice only promotes rot in the tree trunk. Piling stones around trees? Might do some good – but encourages 'ants or pismires'. Water provides plants with 'but a feeble, and weake nourishment, crude, and cold'. Causes moss to grow, too. Companion planting to improve quality? 'I cannot conceive that those things mentioned (or the like), would succeed to the purpose.' And so forth. Poor Bacon.

Yet while there is a great temptation to sympathize wholeheartedly with Austen in his battle against the manifold foolishnesses in *Sylva Sylvarum*, I find myself frequently coming down on Bacon's side. If he got things wrong from time to time – or more often – almost certainly no one else of his period would have done better. It's only fair to recognize what a vast amount of basic knowledge we blithely take for granted four hundred years on — and how hard-won it must have been, largely thanks to curious and persistent men like Bacon. In any event, as his clerical editor Rawley points out, Sir Francis was a man who believed in searching out the true causes of things by means of 'continual conversation with nature and experience', a process in which mistakes were inevitable. Even Austen admitted that at least Bacon's misconceptions 'smell[ed] more of the garden, than the Library'. Bacon himself didn't much care; his mind was on higher things. 'Let no one be concerned,' he once wrote, 'if our history has its errors.'

treat it that way – one company is prepared to wine and dine your VIP guests at the show at up to £450 per head (including ticket).

Ordinary people go there to enjoy themselves, have a little look around, spot a new variety of *Viburnum plicatum*, perhaps, or simply ooh and aah over the show gardens ('How on earth did they get that chrysanthemum to bloom in May?'). Spectacle is of course part of it. But wandering around the great barn (tent no longer), I got the distinct impression that the whole affair might be going somewhere dubious, like over the top.

For one thing, there's the scale. The day is obviously long past when a grower could rent a couple of square yards of space, set up a few tables, cover them with oilcloth or green baize, and spread out an array of interesting plants. Now he has to build a half-scale version of Warwick Castle, muffle it in full-grown trees, lay out flagged paths set in real turf, and toss in a waterfall or two for sound effect. The plants, I suppose, are still the main event, but you can't help but wonder.

Perhaps it's the simple result of competition. The world of commerce is demanding, and these exhibitors are out to sell. Fair enough. As a consumer, however, I find it unsettling. There are still some displays pleasingly proportioned to human beings, but do we really need a vertical half-acre of sweetpeas to convince us that the grower is on our side in the battle against weeds and drought? I'm willing to believe that a professional is capable of laying out a perfectly smashing 'water feature' (cascades, rock pools, bog plants from the Zambezi Basin) on my hillside in Wales without having to prove it by doing the same thing under the monster roof at Chelsea. The effort must be appalling. You could probably mulch half of Hyde Park with the amount of composted bark on view.

I enjoy the outdoor show gardens. Vast ingenuity clearly goes into thinking up ever more spectacular effects and unlikely

[59]

conjunctions, and from time to time a designer comes up with an idea that really inspires you. The desperate pressure to be original occasionally backfires, but outdoors the megalomania is at least muted. Maybe that's because there's less space.

The problem arises when you consider the basic principle at work. A show garden is a show off garden, a sort of horticultural Potemkin village. Every plant will necessarily be at its peak of attractiveness — flowers blooming, groundcovers crisp, climbers climbing gracefully, grasses swishing in the wind exactly the way they are supposed to. Any poor specimen that doesn't measure up hasn't got a hope.

To say that this is unreal is an understatement. Supernatural is more like it. My delphiniums don't bloom at the same time as my tulips. Daffodils have had their day by the time the peonies open. By defeating these laws of nature the show gardens at Chelsea may well create effects that are nothing less than stunning, but if I had the greenest thumb in world (and I don't), *I* couldn't do it. You couldn't either.

And this is where I get hung up. I like to garden, and have increasingly painful doubts that Chelsea is about gardening as I know it and enjoy it. Given that the show is more popular than ever — virtually sold out even before opening — my position may be quixotic, but just possibly Chelsea's very popularity is telling us something. Just as gardening has become enormously fashionable in Britain, it may at the same time started losing touch, in a small and hard-to-grasp way, with its earthy, plant-sized essentials.

I'm not about to give up on the show. Gardening has survived a lot in the past few centuries, and no doubt it will survive a bit of glitz. Don't let that precocious chrysanthemum fool you, though.

EXOTICA

waterlogged because the drainage is so good; and the spears grow straight because the mixture is free of stones and uniform. I figure I have reason to be proud of it.

Meanwhile, the plants in the original bed, which haven't been told what they are missing, go on loyally producing spears. They taste just fine, and I'm not sure how to break the news that their time is almost up.

Freebies

We ought to be grateful to plants that seed themselves. They willingly save us a certain amount of labour, not to mention the cost of those brightly coloured packets that we order with such abandon in the dog days of winter, and then lose track of until the correct time of sowing is well past. Self-seeders don't wait for an idle weekend with no football on television. They don't tergiversate over location (Is there too much shade next to the lilacs? Will the colour clash with the thalictrums?). They simply get on with it, generating offspring with an insouciance that would stagger a welfare department if such a bureaucracy existed in the horticultural world.

Theoretically, it would be possible to have a garden composed completely of self-seeders. To this end I made a list of the plants we can depend on at Towerhill Cottage to reproduce themselves without human intervention, ignoring for the sake of decency outright weeds like thistles and docks and dandelions and ash seedlings. (No, I know you can't ignore them. Weeds are the main reason why an all-self-seeded garden is an impracticality. Anyhow . . .)

First, in terms of both season and prominence, must be the forget-me-nots. As if to make sure we won't, forget-me-nots turn up everywhere – under the *Cornus controversa*, billowing blue in all the beds, covering the floor of the pergola (where they grow in the tiniest pocket of dust or crack between the paving stones). We tend to leave them be, at least until they decline into scruffiness after four or five weeks. By that time, of course, they have ripened and shed their seed, all ready to go next year. (They have also by that time put paid to much of the cement grouting of the paving.)

Probably the most pervasive self-seeders I've had the mixed pleasure of dealing with is the *Alchemilla mollis*. Back in America I regarded alchemilla as something pretty special, which of course it was, being less than keen about our hot dry summers. At first I was happy to protect the ones Carol introduced into the old garden when we bought our house in Wales. Then I began noticing how many of those little round leave were appearing all over the place, in the borders and even among the flagstones, quite unbidden. I was forced to change my mind. Not that alchemilla can't be charming, sometimes; the way drops of water cling like glass beads to its full-grown leaves almost makes me forgive its ubiquity. But I don't want a garden composed of nothing else, and if I gave way, I'm convinced that's what I soon would have. Besides, the self-sown plants are so hard to uproot that they must have larger ambitions in mind.

I certainly don't mean to suggest that all my self-seeders are thugs and marauders. On the contrary, I am delighted to welcome most of them. Our aquilegias are a case in point. They are most likely wild, or the descendants of some unimaginably ancient garden escapee. But they are semi-domesticated, like our cats, and tend to hang around the house and the flowerbeds instead of striking out into the meadow or the woods. You never quite know where they will appear – among the flagstones on the terrace, next to a rose bush on the vegetable garden fence, right in the middle of a sprawling *Chaenomeles japonica* – throwing up a 2-

foot pillar of handsome lobed leaves topped by a cluster of nodding yellow or dark blue 'granny's bonnets'. The bees love them, and I have to admit to being fond of them too.

How self-seeders end up where they do is sometimes, but not always, a mystery. *Limnanthes douglasii* (better known as poached egg flower) seeds itself wherever you first plant it, naturally enough; the mystery in this case is how it survives when the whole area involved has been carefully weeded late in the fall and again in the spring. Love-in-a-mist (*Nigella damascena*) displays more of a wanderlust, probably because the seeds are so tiny and so impressively numerous, but with us it tends to fill up its own patch first, crowding it with seedlings to the point where its hard to believe anything could grow. I could thin them, but I've found that there is no real need. You get a nice stand of pale blue blossoms from the winners, while the losers simply contribute to the mist. And there are always a few strays in other places where you don't expect them.

Certain self-seeders seem destined to continue on into eternity, not in huge numbers like the nigellas, but enough to maintain the family line. Eight or ten years ago I started some *Verbena bonariensis* from a packet of seed, impressed by the attention being paid to the plant in gardening magazines. No garden could be authentically *au courant*, so it was said, without a copse of these great gawks showing off their small purplish panicles four feet in mid-air. Whether or not we achieved the desired stylishness is a moot point, but from that day to this *V. bonariensis* has been familiar inhabitant, seeding itself with some precision into just those places where it has a fair chance of surviving the spring clean-up. Its thin poles are consequently rather scattered now, which detracts a bit from the original effect. In fact, these days the usual reaction of visitors to our *V. bonariensis* is less often admiration than a startled 'What's *that*?' especially when they come face to face (literally) with one growing in the middle of a paved path.

You cannot, however, take self-seeders for granted. Some simply won't perform the way the books say they are supposed to. I've been trying for ages to get ox-eye daisies (*Leucanthemum vulgare*) – reputedly great self-seeders – to naturalize in my wild meadow, with no luck. (Maybe the grass is too powerful.) The same goes for several other wildflower species. On the other hand, we get hellebores in all sorts of places where we don't want them (including the meadow), pansies and lychnis (*L. coronaria*) popping up indiscriminately and globe thistles (*Echinops*) gradually colonizing the last 10 feet of what was meant to be a bed shared with hollyhocks and artichokes. Any conceivable demand for those handsome all-green euphorbias (*Euphorbia amygdaloides* var. *robbiae*) may be satisfied by the crop seeding itself so vigorously in the brick paving around the front door that getting into the house becomes problematical. The same might be said for the eryngium known as 'Miss Willmott's Ghost' (*E. giganteum*) if only it would consent to being transplanted from the awkward place it has chosen to settle, in the cracks between the flagstones on the terrace. Dig it out, it dies.

Of all the self-seeders enjoying themselves – and mostly pleasing us – around our garden, there is one that is a particular torment and a delight. I'm not sure where our first samples of annual edging lobelia (*L. erinus*) came from – probably a planting in one of the stone troughs a decade ago – but every year now they seed themselves between the terrace flagstones. When I first laid those stones, I butted them as tightly as possible. Even so, cracks remained, and this space regularly fills with a mixture of larch needles, earth, worm casts and, inevitably, weeds. The latter must be scraped out every spring using one of my favourite tools, a flat metal hook with a yellow plastic handle that is always falling off. Now, as anyone must know who has ever tried to preserve infant self-seeded plants in a flowerbed in spring while at the same time disposing of chickweed, grass, dandelions, nettles, daisies and all the other pests a garden is heir to, it's a tricky business. I can testify that it is even trickier when the desired seedlings are a quarter of an inch high, practically invisible and in any case almost indistinguishable from everything else growing between the stones. You need to move slowly, with great care, and accept the fact that you are most likely slaughtering every third lobelia. The job takes days, but it's worth it. The payoff comes in August and lasts until frost – a dusting of gleaming blue across the old red sandstone flags.

What more could be asked of any plant, self-seeder or otherwise?

The Leaf Blower

Very few gardening activities can be quite so boring, exhausting, and pointless as raking leaves. Does anybody enjoy it? If the leaves are wet (and they usually are in autumn in Wales), they cling to the lawn like cats' paws; if they are dry, the wind sends them flying right back to where they were raked from. With only modest success I have tried over the years to hire somebody else to do the job for me. It is a job that certainly needs to be done — we have an exceptional number of trees, nearly all deciduous. Even the conifers — the larches, anyway — insist on shedding their greenery as winter approaches.

Over the years I have tried a number of leaf-gathering solutions. The most successful (apart from the neighbourhood boy who finally realized that there were easier ways to earn five quid) was the rotary lawnmower. If you managed matters correctly (and didn't need to deal with too many — or too wet — leaves) it was possible, I found, to employ the mower as a sort of lawn broom. Running over a few leaves, it pitched them out the side along with the cut grass, shredding them in the process. Of course you eventually had to rake up the windrows of leaves/grass, a moderately strenuous process.

So I became the owner of a leaf blower.

It wasn't the first piece of garden machinery I've bought. On the contrary, as I've explained elsewhere I have quite a collection – a string trimmer, a chainsaw, a hedge clipper, a rototiller, that mower, and several others big and small. I frankly delight in them. They save a vast amount of time and labour. Purists (like organic gardeners) might argue that I'm missing some of perks concomitant to hand work – for example that sense of ecstatic close-to-the-earth weariness granted to those who have put in a solid day's toil with a bucksaw or a hoe. But if weariness is the issue, I don't have any problem getting weary lifting a twenty-pound hedge clipper over sixty yards of hedge.

I got my leaf blower toward the end of last autumn, having already finished collecting most of the year's leaves with a rake. I used the blower only a few times, experimentally you might say, to corral some late-descending leaves and to see whether it might not serve to clear the grass cuttings inadvertently sprayed on the gravel drive by the lawnmower. It worked all too well on the drive – it blew both grass cuttings and a substantial proportion of the gravel straight back on to the lawn. As for the leaves, the main problem was getting them into a pile, since the blower functioned rather like a stiff north-east wind, with about the same degree of discrimination. Before long it went into winter storage.

It was at this point that I started wondering about the history of this device. It must, I thought, be a fairly recent invention. The first time I ever saw one, I couldn't figure out what it was. That was about 1990 in a big hardware store in Troy, New York. Since then I've seldom seen them in Britain; Monnow Mowers and Machinery in Monmouth, where I got mine, has been carrying them for only a few years. So I decided to do some leaf blower research. What I discovered makes me wonder whether I'll ever have the nerve to use it again. This is a machine in very deep controversy, if not worse.

According to most sources, leaf blowers were invented by Japanese engineers in the 1970s, and originally used to blow fertilizers and pesticides over fruit trees and grain fields. A container of chemicals sat atop a powerful fan, to be blasted in the general direction of a needy crop through a nozzle. One day somebody discovered that even without the chemicals, the blast of air alone could be of use, and the leaf blower was born. Imaginative manufacturers have since come up with more uses for the machine than ever would have occurred to me, such as blowing snow, emptying rain gutters, cleaning parking lots and sports arenas, 'dislodging matted grass' (whatever that is), 'drying lawns' and, of course, gathering leaves. Some leaf blowers, I learn, can be made to run backwards, thus creating a kind of outdoor Hoover capable of sucking up leaves and other debris. An admittedly arcane use involved scientists studying lizard locomotion in the Mojave Desert, who found that a leaf blower was the best way to smooth the sand at night.

Now while this range of practical applications doesn't quite make the machines a benefit to humanity on the level of, say, penicillin or mains electricity, it does suggest that most people would regard them as admirable. Thus I was surprised to find that leaf blowers are not much loved. In fact, in many places in the United States, especially California, they are not even tolerated. Within three years of their introduction, the chic Pacific coast resort of Carmel had banned them, and Beverley Hills was not far behind. Today six out of the ten largest California cities either ban leaf blowers outright or place severe restrictions on their use. This in spite of the fact that according to the latest figures I've been able to find (1999) something like one million petrol and electric leaf blowers have been sold in California alone. Nor can leaf-blower rage, like so many other eccentricities, be written off as a peculiarly Californian phenomenon. New Jersey and Arizona have both considered state-level laws against the machines, while prosperous Montgomery County in Maryland has had a restrictive law on the books for fifteen years. Five other states have at least one city with a leaf blower ordinance.

What's the fuss? Plenty, if you listen to the protestors. One objection is the amount of dust – containing everything from pollen to pesticide – that leaf blowers create, no doubt a worse problem in hot, dry Southern California than in Wales. Then, so far as petrol-powered blowers are concerned, there are the engine emissions; generally speaking, a two-stroke engine spews nearly a third of its fuel unburned into the air, adding to pollution. (This failing naturally applies equally to petrol engines driving most garden machinery, from chainsaws to lawnmowers – for this reason they are also under attack in some quarters, often in the same restrictive legislation.) But the heart of the problem is noise.

It is difficult to describe precisely the noise made by a leaf blower running at full throttle. It is a sort of deep, hollow roar, a sound that wraps itself around your spine and causes synapses to misfire. I once had a model jet engine that made a noise like that. When I ran it in our neighbourhood park, kids came from miles around to see what was going on. So wearing ear protectors while operating a blower is not only a good idea, it's imperative.

Most of the ordinances controlling leaf blowers (as opposed to banning them) specify that the noise they make should be limited to 65 decibels at 50 feet, variously described as 'the sound of an alarm clock' or 'freeway traffic'. Studies have shown, however, that the average leaf blower emits roughly 110 decibels, which is a great deal louder; a car horn, a pneumatic drill, or somebody shouting in your ear registers about 110 decibels. Experts claim that extended exposure (more than eight hours) to as little as 85 decibels is pretty sure to cause damage to one's hearing.

To their credit (and no doubt to the health of their balance sheets) manufacturers have been looking for ways to minimize noise with better engineering. They have also been active in providing guidelines for behaving responsibly when using leaf blowers (landscaping work gangs should use only one blower at a time, avoid early morning and evening sessions, note which way the dust is blowing, keep the engine throttled down as much as possible – i.e. don't chase a single cigarette butt at full blast). Above all, they have been busy lobbying against controls, sometimes with success – at one point they got a law banning bans introduced in the California State Senate (it was defeated).

At the moment my leaf blower is hanging in the barn, gleaming quietly, its black plastic nozzle ready to roar at the pull of a starter cord. Autumn is approaching, and my enthusiasm for raking is at a serious ebb. The temptation to get out there and blow will, I know, be extremely powerful. Monmouthshire has made no move towards banning the machine and is unlikely to, so I won't be breaking any laws. The question is: should I? I suggest you listen carefully come October. You'll probably be able to hear the answer.

Chelsea

Is it gardening? Or is it gardening gone mad?

We're about to face the Chelsea Flower Show again, and I'm still trying to recover from last year's. It was a knockout. The labour involved on the part of the exhibitors must have been staggering. Certainly the results were. I couldn't begin to detail them, but they included a garden full of 5,000 brightly-coloured metal spheres on sticks (for sale at £300,000), another with a bomb crater in it, a modest affair featuring 40 tonnes of firewood and pavers shipped from Melbourne, immense amounts of decking, tea pavilions, a papier maché tortoise, and about 10 million plants – far too many to shake a hoe at, anyway. It was an awe-inspiring sight.

Chelsea is regarded as the epitome of British gardening and, as everybody knows, British gardening is the model for the rest of the world. So it may be worth pausing for moment in the breathless rush of admiration to ask what's going on here. Do these endless ranks of perfect streptocarpus, these towers of terracotta and legions of lavender, these climbing and creeping and billowing roses have anything to do with the rest of us, pottering with enthusiasm but modest skill around our equally modest gardens?

It might be argued that Chelsea is supposed to be something of a circus, like Ascot. Certainly the corporate entertainment outfits

Ferme Ornée

Whether it's scarlet blossoms in the bean patch or roses on the rabbit fence, or maybe a nice selection of salad greens and herbs arranged for aesthetic as well as gustatory pleasure just outside the kitchen door, most gardens share elements of the beautiful and the useful. This comes naturally; there's no need to elevate the idea into a design principle.

During one of the odder and shortest-lived phases of gardening history, however, a few English gentlemen undertook to do just that. They invented the *ferme ornée* ('embellished' or 'ornamented' farm), which proposed to celebrate the charms of working rural life with all the artifices of the garden designer. Beauty and utility would go hand in hand, cows with campanulas, vistas with bleating sheep. That this was a half-baked idea was not immediately apparent. In fact, before the fad had run its course two such farms had become famous throughout Britain, visited and discussed by thousands of garden-lovers.

The first was begun about 1734 by Philip Southcote near Chertsey in Surrey. Southcote, at thirty-four, had married the seventy-year-old dowager Duchess of Cleveland, bringing himself a comfortable marriage settlement of £16,000 (nearly £1 million today). He promptly prevailed upon his prosperous bride to buy Woburn (or Wooburn) Farm for him, a 125-acre spread containing the usual appurtenances of cattles, sheep, chickens, pastures and arable land, and went to work converting it into something new and strange.

Historians differ about Southcote's originality. Certainly writers such as Batty Langley, author of *New Principles of Gardening*, had recommended making 'a beautiful Rural Garden' out of the elements of a farm several years earlier. And the use of the French term suggests European antecedents. But Woburn was the first real *ferme ornée* to be built, and unquestionably the first to achieve fame.

The best description of Southcote's creation occurs in a contemporary garden tour guide, *Observations on Modern Gardening*, by Thomas Whately. The ornamented portion of Woburn, occupying in all about 35 acres, seems to have consisted of a broad irregular walkway circling the whole farm. 'This walk is properly garden,' writes Whately; 'all within it is farm; the whole lies on the two sides of a hill, and on a flat at the foot of it: the flat is divided into cornfields; the pastures occupy the hill; they are surrounded by the walk, and crossed by a communication carried along the brow, which is also richly dressed, and which divides them into two lawns, each completely encompassed with garden.' Carefully placed groves of trees, a few decorative buildings, 'little seats, alcoves, and bridges', and what must have been miles of perennial borders, hedges filled with 'odoriferous plants', flowering shrubs and other high-maintenance delights completed the ensemble. Whately, while admiring Woburn, expressed some doubts – the plantings, especially of flowers, struck him as excessive ('the variety [would be] more pleasing, had it been less licentious'), and though the farm was very much a working affair, its essential 'rusticity of character' had been lost in a 'profusion of ornament'. In other words, Southcote had overdone it.

It is worth noting that Southcote seems to have placed a relatively low emphasis on ornamenting buildings. Woburn's normal farm buildings – and the main house – existed, of course, and use was made of neighbouring steeples and bridges as focal points for views. But the gardens were what made it a *ferme ornée*.

Similarly, the poet William Shenstone's Leasowes, probably the best known *ferme ornée* ever built, possessed a fairly ordinary house, along with a barn or two retained largely for the sake of calling the place a *ferme* at all. The encircling walk, the ruins (some real), the cascades and pools, the groves and urns and inscribed monuments, all the paraphernalia of a romantic if slightly gimcrack Arcady, were what Shenstone enjoyed and concentrated upon. He was at heart a romantic, no kind of farmer at all, a plump bachelor with a taste for social climbing and fashionable verse.

It was in about 1743 that he took possession of the 150-acre farm near Birmingham that his grandfather had purchased some years earlier. In contrast to Southcote, Shenstone was not rich. Having only £300 a year to work with, he had to scrabble to fund his visions of rural bliss (£4 a year came from renting his ruined priory to an elderly couple). But he was imaginative and ambitious, willing to plant and excavate with the best of them. The result was a sort of theoretical paradise, less a farm than a highly artificial series of perspectives complete with livestock.

Like Woburn, the Leasowes featured a garden belt wandering across and around the estate, with specific beauty spots indicated *en route*. We know a great deal about its exact layout because of Shenstone's thirst for publicity; most of the prominent people of the time, from Samuel Johnson to John Wesley to a raft of noblemen, paid the Leasowes a visit, and often wrote glowingly about it afterwards. Mrs Thrale even broke into verse:

To Shenstone in his grot retired
My truest praise I'll pay;
And view with just contempt inspired
The glitter of the gay.

Shenstone himself admitted that his *ferme ornée* 'procures me interviews with persons whom it might otherwise be my wish rather than my good-fortune to see'. And his publisher Robert Dodsley, not missing a promotional trick, appended a full description and a detailed map of the Leasowes to his edition of Shenstone's *Collected Poems*.

Well-received as they were, Woburn Farm and the Leasowes seem to have attracted few followers. Landed proprietors with space and money to spare were apparently less inclined to embellish a farm than to call on the services of a man like 'Capability' Brown – just then coming into prominence – to create an impressive landscape. Compared to a grand Brownian sweep of trees and lawns, a mere farm lacked drama.

Curiously, though, the term *ferme ornée* did not die out, but gradually metamorphosed. On the one hand, it began to be applied to beautified farmhouses, cottages (the *cottage ornée*), and other structures without any particular reference to gardens; in 1795 a writer named John Plaw published a handbook of designs under the title of *The Ferme Ornée or Rural Improvements*. On the other hand, it was used in connection with large working estates such as George Washington's Mount Vernon and Thomas Jefferson's Monticello, which although they combined handsome houses with agricultural enterprises were a far cry from the precious elegancies of Shenstone. Jefferson himself seems to have bridled at the reference, regarding the English *ferme ornée* as insufficiently practical.

It was in America that remnants of the basic idea lingered on, well into the nineteenth century, in the work of the great horticulturist, landscapist and architect A.J. Downing. 'The embellished farm (*ferme ornée*) is a pretty mode of combining something of the beauty of the landscape with the utility of the farm,' he wrote, 'and we hope to see small country seats of this kind become more general.' To this end Downing offered layout designs featuring curving drives, oddly shaped fields, and 'tasteful' farmhouses. The prime example of the Downing *ferme ornée*, however, was a vast estate built for the magnate Matthew Vassar in Poughkeepsie, New York, with plantings, picturesque buildings, carriage drives, gardens – and only incidentally a farm.

In 1828, Woburn Farm was reported to be 'now completely obliterated, and the grounds let as a common farm'. They are now occupied by a college. The gardens of the Leasowes did not outlive Shenstone by much; the property, surrounded by urban development, eventually became a golf course. Today, the Dudley Metropolitan Borough Council has ambitious plans in the works to restore it to its eighteenth-century state.

The Age of Guano

One warm evening in August 1830, a sea captain named Smith exhibited a small pile of brownish yellow powder to a meeting of the Massachusetts Horticultural Society in Boston. It was, so the Society's historian later recorded, 'a kind of manure from Peru, called by the Spaniards "guano", then a novelty here.'

Guano did not remain a novelty for long. It was already being talked about, and within twenty years would be regarded as 'indispensable . . . like a necessary of life to us'. By then the question was no longer whether or not it was an effective fertilizer. Gardeners and farmers in America, Britain and on the Continent were universally convinced of its near-magical powers. The only problem posed by guano, it seemed, was how to get more of it, preferably at an affordable price.

Today, when all manner of chemical fertilizers are readily available for our choosing in the sacks and boxes and bottles lined up in long rows in every garden centre, it is difficult to imagine the enthusiasm, bordering on desperation, with which guano was received. The demand was enormous. In fact, over the relatively short course of what we may call the Age of Guano, this pungently unattractive substance was responsible for trade wars and shooting wars, the creation of monopolies, smuggling, huge profits, the passage of laws, diplomatic contretemps and considerable cruelties, to say nothing of forgery and other fakery on a large scale. But it also ushered in the modern system of intensive cultivation and the use of artificial fertilizers. Not a small achievement for a pile of bird dung.

Because that's exactly what guano is. For hundreds of thousands of years, on a variety of off-shore rocks and small islands where sea birds roost and breed, their droppings built up and dried into layers sometimes hundreds of feet thick. In the case of the best guano, that found on the Chincha Islands just off Peru, all of the main elements required by plants – nitrogen, phosphorus and potassium – are present in concentrated and readily available form. Peruvian farmers had made use of guano from time immemorial, but it was not until 1804, when the explorer Alexander Humboldt brought a sample back to Germany and had it tested by chemists and a potato-growing English friend on the island of St Helena, that anyone in the outside world had an inkling of its virtues. And even then these virtues were mysterious. A basic understanding of plant chemistry was still lacking, and would be until the German scientist Justus von Liebig finally published his *Organic Chemistry in Its Application to Agriculture and Physiology* in 1840.

What was clear to many farmers was that *something* had to be done to restore the dwindling fertility of their soil. Certain particularly voracious crops such as tobacco and cotton had reduced the value of many farms in the American mid-Atlantic and southern states to practically nothing. In the older states in the north, matters were scarcely better. In the once-rich Genesee valley of New York State, for example, average corn yields had dropped from 30 bushels an acre in 1775 to 8 in 1845. In England, farmers were discovering that traditional farmyard manure was simply not adequate to boost the production of turnips, an absolutely basic crop. All sorts of fertilizers came in for trial, from salt to sawdust to bones, but with few exceptions the results were disappointing.

The first small shipments of guano, a few casks, began trickling into the United States and England in the 1830s. Results of tests in both countries were exciting. Before long a combine of English and Peruvian businessmen had secured a monopoly on mining and shipping guano from the Chincha Islands, and the rest of the globe was being scavenged for other sources.

Everybody wanted it. In England, the Earl of Derby bought a whole shipload and was so delighted by the result that he became a propagandist for guano. In Virginia, a farmer reported growing wheat 'high enough to hide a dog' on exhausted land that had been treated with 200 pounds of guano per acre; wheat on the neighbouring untreated field 'wouldn't hide a chicken – not even an egg'. The Prague Agricultural Society began promoting its use, and in upstate New York, the Shaker seedsmen of New Lebanon discovered that guano not only increased production but improved the quality 'of seeds of all descriptions . . . to an astonishing degree'. It did wonders for turnips and was even said to bring on repeat flowering in roses.

Fortunately, too, a little guano went a long way. This meant that it could be used on fields too remote to be fertilized with bulky farmyard manure. But it had its drawbacks. It was tricky to handle – gardeners and farmers were advised to avoid breathing the dust, and at least one man died when he inadvertently swallowed some. The worst drawback, however, was the cost.

In 1842, the Peruvian government nationalized its guano resources, and thereafter effectively controlled the price. Peruvian was the choicest variety – unlike competing guanos discovered elsewhere, off Africa, in the Caribbean and the Pacific, it retained a high nitrogen content because of the rainless climate where it was formed. The British monopoly-holders shipped most of it to England and the Continent, making enormous profits; what little reached the United States was increasingly expensive too.

It was a recipe for trouble. In both Britain and America, frauds blossomed like chickweed as ingenious shysters pushed adulterated versions spiked with sawdust, rice, meal, chalk, sulphates of lime or magnesia, salt, sand, earth, peat or water. Low-grade guano that never saw the Chincha Islands passed as blue-ribbon stuff, while agricultural manuals warned buyers to 'buy none but Peruvian' and offered simple tests supposed to reveal fakes. But the demand continued – according to some estimates, up to the 1850s four times as much Peruvian guano could have been sold in the United States as was available.

There were inevitable political repercussions. At one point in 1852, a Boston businessman with empty ships returning from Gold Rush California caused an international incident by attempting to load Peruvian guano without permission from some islands up the coast from the Chinchas. (He was discouraged by a Peruvian gunboat.) There were protests in Parliament about price-fixing, and year after year farm interests pressured the United States government to do something to bring down the cost. It was all to little effect; neither Peru nor the monopolists had reason to make concessions when the money was flowing in at such a rate. Only brute force – a military seizure – might do the trick, and nobody was up to that. According to historian Jimmy Skaggs, by 1856 Congressional committees had investigated the guano problem no less than nine times. The upshot was the passage in that year of an extraordinary piece of legislation. The Guano Islands Act (which incidentally remains in effect to this day) was intended to encourage the discovery and exploitation of deposits other than Peruvian by giving any American finding one the right to it on a monopoly basis – with the claim backed up by the US Navy if necessary.

The Act led to claims on dozens of islets and reefs around the world, incidentally projecting an American presence all the way across the Pacific. It also led to the production of a good deal of guano, though of a kind less desirable than the Peruvian because its nitrogen had been leached out. By this time, however, the fertilizer world was changing. New ways of making artificial varieties and of stepping up the potency of more common substances such as rock phosphates meant that demand for high-priced prime guano was falling off. British farmers were beginning to realize that cheaper sorts were perfectly good for turnips, which didn't need the nitrogen. And it was becoming obvious that the magic powder was not the whole answer; such old-fashioned supplements as animal manure were also needed to maintain a good soil structure.

In any case, the Chinchas were running out. Vast as the original guano deposits had been ('inexhaustible', said one confident observer in 1853), over the course of thirty years more than ten million tons had been excavated and shipped abroad, often under extremely unpleasant conditions, by ill-paid or slave labourers. The trade brought vast sums into the Peruvian treasury – estimates range up to nearly £20 million (over £1 billion today) during the 1850s alone – whence it was for the most part corruptly siphoned out again. In 1864, a newly bellicose Spain seized the islands from Peru and held them for two years. Finally, in 1868, shipments from the Chinchas ceased. The Age of Guano was coming to an end. By 1910 an agricultural scientist could write that 'guano is now largely a manure of the past'.

Still, it was a long time before the term guano dropped out of common use among gardeners and farmers. Most early twentieth century garden guides mention it, although the substance itself was no longer widely available. The real thing is still being produced in small quantities on the Chinchas under conrolled conditions aimed at protecting the seabirds' nesting cycle, mainly for Peruvian use. Elsewhere around the world a few deposits are being worked, but most of the first-rate nitrogenous guano is gone. Some claims under the American Guano Islands Act have had exotic subsequent histories — at least one in the Caribbean ended up as a secret CIA base shipping arms into Nicaragua. As recently as 1998 a Californian entrepreneur laid claim under the Act to Navassa Island, an uninhabited rock near Haiti that was long ago the scene of a murderous uprising by guano miners; it is unclear whether he intends to excavate guano or hunt sunken treasure, possibly both. Although the deposit is distinctly marginal so far as quality goes, there's said to be a market for Navassa guano in the citrus orchards of Florida.

Publishing the Garden

I suppose people in other countries also get exercised about hedges, but one thing is certain: you have to come to Britain to get a real feel for the kind of internecine warfare such growths can cause. Scarcely a month goes by without yet another newspaper story of a fight to the death over a hedge that has been allowed to get out of control. Sometimes the death is of the hedge; unfortunately often it's of the hedge-owner – or, worse, the hedge-owner's poor etiolated neighbour.

Desperate to calm the situation, the government recently acted. Inserted in the 2003 Antisocial Behaviour Act is a clause that makes it possible to apply to the local council for adjudication of a conflict over an offending hedge. Whether this will work or not remains to be seen; the proprietor might claim that the hedge is necessary as a windbreak, or to protect his privacy, or (for all I know) to supply his family with hazelnuts in the winter, and get away with it. In any case, you can't begin to complain until the hedge is more than two metres high. Moreover, it has to be a proper evergreen or semi-evergreen hedge – single trees, however lofty and light-excluding, don't come under the Act. Nor do such things as bamboos or beech, no matter how they are planted.

Frankly, as an American I have always regarded British hedge-rage as inevitable. It's built into the social ethos. In a country where enclosure is the norm, combined with an inbred urge to make things grow, trouble between neighbours is anything but surprising. It doesn't even need to involve hedges – I note in today's paper a report of a fracas between two adjacent ladies over a *Clematis montana* on a shared fence; before they ended up in court one of them had attacked the other with a wheelbarrow, while the clematis had suffered a presumably mortal scissoring.

At the heart of the matter, of course, is the British love of privacy, the national insistence on building walls, green or otherwise, around whatever small or large piece of God's earth he or she can lay claim to. I've written about this before, and after twenty years in the UK I've come to regard it as almost normal. Besides, I like privacy as much as the next man. What has begun to seem stranger to me is the American practice of no enclosure at all around one's property, just lawns running into lawns, interrupted only by the odd driveway, tree or flowerbed.

I've always assumed (maybe rightly) that the American taste for openness stemmed originally from our horror of forests. The first settlers must have been eager to clear a space that sunlight could reach. They needed to plant crops, and a clear view of their neighbours was no doubt comforting. Moreover, fencing was expensive, the sort of thing you used only to keep wandering cows out of your vegetables. The tradition – and you can see it to this day in such venerable (if restored) establishments as the Old Mission House in Stockbridge, Massachusetts, built in 1739 – was for a fenced dooryard garden, private only in the sense that pigs were not admitted. This garden would have a few lilacs, herbs for the kitchen and perhaps – depending on the ambitions and spare time of the householder – some flowers. Even after the frontier moved west into the treeless prairies, the same pattern held, at least well into the nineteenth century.

But was it fixed for good? Were American householders destined always to conduct their lives in full view of their neighbours, to say nothing of every snoop wandering down the street? It never occurred to me to think otherwise until I ran across a splendid anthology called *The American Gardener*, put together by Allen Lacy. It contains, along with a lot of other provocative material, extracts from several writers who felt strongly about precisely this issue. To say that they were at odds with each other would be putting it mildly.

For example Neltje Blanchan, who believed in privacy, argued that 'the family life that should be lived as much as possible under the open sky, when rudely exposed to public gaze, must become either vulgarly brazen or sensitively shy'. The only solution to this abhorrent prospect, she suggested, was 'an encircling belt of trees' or 'a tall hedge around [the] garden room' (but not, of course, 'the Englishman's insultingly inhospitable brick wall, topped with broken bottles'). Otherwise, 'the perfect freedom of home life is no more possible than if the family living room were to be set on a public stage'. To the New England novelist Sarah Orne Jewett, an open garden 'is like writing down family secrets for anyone to read; it is like having everybody call you by your first name, or sit in any pew in church'.

Some commentators were even more outspoken. George Washington Cable, writing in 1914, associated the American garden's 'excessive openness' with a national wish to be candid and polite. Privacy, he felt, no longer counted for much. 'We seem to enjoy publicity better. In our American eagerness to publish everything for everybody and to everybody, we have published our gardens.' He placed his hope (a faint one, as it turned out) in the newly cheap and available wire fencing, which could serve to delineate boundaries – and at the very least keep out the neighbour's spaniels.

For her part, the prolific garden essayist Alice Morse Earle regretted the passing of the fenced dooryard in favour of 'that dreary destroyer of a garden . . . the desire for a lawn'. There is a note of nostalgia here, and of despair – the fact is that for decades before she wrote (in 1901), the lawn had already become the central feature of the typical American home garden, especially in small towns and on the edges of cities. The invention of the lawnmower encouraged it. Lawns and openness went together. In one of the most influential books of the period, *The Art of Beautifying Suburban Home Grounds* (1870), Frank J. Scott spelled out the point: 'A smooth, closely shaven surface of grass is by far the most essential element of beauty on the grounds of a suburban house.' Trees are important too, but 'it requires half a lifetime to obtain them, while the lawn may be perfected in two or three years'.

In Scott's view, moreover, the lawn – and all the other horticultural delights produced by the assiduous gardener – must never be hidden away behind 'walls, high fences, hedge screens and belts of trees and shrubbery *which are used for that purpose only*'. In his forcefully expressed opinion, 'It is unchristian to hedge from the sight of others the beauties of nature which it has been our good fortune to create or secure.' To do so, as the English do, would be 'as unfortunate to follow as it would be to imitate the surly self-assertiveness of English travelling manners'. To Scott, if not to Robert Frost, good fences don't make good neighbours. Good neighbours are the product of no fences at all.

Driving through the suburbs of Detroit or Chicago, or any of a thousand small cities across the Midwest, it is plain to see that Frank Scott won the argument, such as it was. Sophisticated gardens today may have their garden rooms, plenty of old trees have grown up to shade the footpaths and front porches, and flowerbeds and shrubberies nowadays often interrupt the lawns. Hedges of privet or barberry are hardly unknown. But there is rarely an attempt at real privacy in the British style, with leylandii, hornbeam and yew.

Nor, so far as I know, is there much hedge-rage, either.

Pineta

To gardeners, evergreens have always had a particular charm. In the 1660s, for example, John Evelyn planned and planted a special grove on his estate at Deptford. Even in the bleak depths of an English winter, he figured, there would be greenery to look at.

Evelyn was ahead of his time. The choice of conifers available to him was still fairly limited – two or three types of pine, the Norway spruce, the silver fir, the yew, a few others – and he had to fall back on shrubs and groundcovers to fill out his planting. It would be more than a hundred years before the exploits of plant hunters began to reveal the true riches of the world of evergreens, especially the conifers growing on the Pacific Coast of North America. And this would in turn eventually touch off a fad for a garden feature that Evelyn might well have admired and envied: the pinetum.

Technically, according to Edward Luckhurst, a professional gardener writing in 1873, 'a complete pinetum consists of a collection of one or more of each variety of Conifer that is worthy of cultivation'. As a number of contemporary examples showed, this could be an ambitious target indeed.

Until the end of the eighteenth century, almost the only foreign 'pine' (all conifers were for a long time called pines – and so were, confusingly, pineapples) known in Britain was the cedar of Lebanon. 'Capability' Brown planted no other non-native species in his grand landscaping schemes. In 1792, however, a naval expedition coasting north to Alaska reported seeing enormous trees of an unknown kind, and in 1826 the collector David Douglas sent back the first seeds of the Sitka spruce (*Picea sitchensis*). It was the beginning of a flood. Douglas was subsequently responsible for many of the new conifers – most notably the Douglas fir (*Pseudotsuga menzieii*), which can grow over 300 feet tall – before his remarkable demise in Hawaii. He fell into a wild bull trap already occupied by an angry wild bull.

But there were still more trees and still more collectors. Sawara and Hinoki cypresses came from Japan; the deodar cedar from the Western Himalayas, grown from a seed brought back in 1831; *Cryptomeria* from China; firs, pines and spruces from the Pacific Coast. The bizarre monkey puzzle tree (*Araucaria araucana*) arrived from Chile, the Norfolk Island pine (really another araucaria, *A. heterophylla*) from the Antipodes. The most splendid tree of all, the enormous wellingtonia (*Sequoiadendron giganteum*) made its ponderous way from California in the 1850s. Soon the choice of conifers was almost overwhelming. One estimate suggests that by the end of the nineteenth century anyone venturing to create a comprehensive pinetum in England might need to find a place for no less than 250 different species.

Nevertheless, many estate owners undertook the challenge, driven by fashion or the pure collector's instinct. The size of their pineta might range from a few dozen to many hundreds of trees, and from obvious, simply grown species to recalcitrant rarities. It usually depended on the wealth of the proprietor and the space available ('avoid all approaches to crowding', counselled Luckhurst). Thus by the 1860s such ducal spreads as Chatsworth could boast particularly fine pineta, while scarcely less impressive ones could be found in other rich men's gardens – places like

Elvaston Castle, Bicton, Woburn Abbey or Dropmore. But in fact nearly every self-respecting country mansion possessed a pinetum of some sort.

At Elvaston, the pinetum was divided into two sections, one composed of pines and the other of firs and spruces. An avenue cut through each section, and plantings were arranged along the avenues so that taller trees stood behind the shorter ones – a row of Irish yews in front, then a row of golden yews, then araucarias, and finally deodars grafted on cedars of Lebanon. 'If any artificial assemblage of trees can reach the sublime in gardening, this . . . is no mean example of one,' wrote a gobstruck visitor. The head gardener responsible for Elvaston, William Barron, not incidentally became famous for his skill in moving large trees. Probably his greatest achievement was to dig up and move a huge 800-year-old yew from a churchyard – without killing it.

Contemporary enthusiasm for pineta was encouraged by the copious writings of John Claudius Loudon, the leading horticultural journalist of his day. Loudon, who had designed the famous Derby Arboretum, was a great tree man and an indefatigable advice-giver on all manner of gardening questions. In his opinion, the correct way to plant trees was on little hills, so as to expose the beauty of their main roots. Significantly, this same tactic was frequently employed in the planting of pineta for other aesthetic reasons. At Biddulph Grange in Staffordshire, where James Bateman began building a highly original and influential garden in 1842, the pinetum was arranged along the sides of a curving walk, with the trees all situated on low mounds. Such a device, noted one visitor, brought 'the beautiful forms . . . between the spectator and the sky, without any intervening background.'

One matter never wholly solved was how the trees should be arranged within the pinetum. Should they be planted symmetrically? By height? By genus? By whatever system makes them look best, or for picturesque effect? At Bowood in 1850 John Spencer created a pinetum by setting out his specimens according to their place of geographic origin. Some critics approved, others were dismayed.

Along with so much else that depends on having a couple of hundred acres to garden in and as many gardeners to do the work, pineta are uncommon today. Biddulph Grange, extensively restored since 1988 and now managed by the National Trust, still has one, and most major arboretums have conifer collections. Some grand old trees survive. But for the most part the pinetum as a garden feature has dissolved, with the firs, spruces, monkey puzzles and the rest no longer segregated but scattered into the broader horticultural community – where they belong.

The Shrinking Violet

In the Victorian era certain plants had a way of insinuating themselves into unexpected realms of popular taste. There was, for example, the fad for water lilies, touched off by the introduction to Britain in 1845 of the gigantic *Victoria amazonica* from the Brazilian backcountry; this led to such extraordinary manifestations as papier maché cradles in the form of lilies, splendidly twining gas fixtures and, ultimately, Art Nouveau. Fashion loved flowers even more, from the cattleyas that enchanted Proust's characters to the imitation roses decorating the most elegant gowns. But even in this botanical company, one small blossom seems to have had an exceptional – if impermanent – impact: the scented violet.

It may be difficult to grasp, especially if like me you are not particularly fond of the smell of violets, the scale and spread of violetophilia in its heyday. At one point no fewer than 300 nurseries along the Hudson north of New York City were growing the plants for cut flowers. In France, as many as six boxcars loaded with bouquets left Toulouse for Paris every evening, while other growers in the Paris suburbs more than doubled the supply. (Records show that growers in the south of France alone produced 13,000 pounds of violets in 1874.) Annually, upwards of a million turquoise and white Parma blossoms made the nine-day train journey from Udine in northern Italy to St Petersburg, remaining in acceptably good condition for another ten days after arrival. Meanwhile more thousands of sweet-smelling bunches were coming up to London from the West Country to fill the baskets of the ubiquitous street-corner violet-sellers. By the 1890s, the violet was the world's third most important flower in commercial terms, exceeded only by roses and carnations.

Where did the fashion start? If you care to be thoroughly antiquarian about it, you might argue that it began with the Greeks, whose enthusiasm for violets was such that they set up nurseries near Athens in the fourth century BC. Medieval herbalists thought a lot of violets for their soporific qualities; the odour obviously had a special appeal in the days of open sewers and infrequent baths. (Its principal element is a chemical called ionine, which has the peculiar property of not only charming the sense of smell, but of deadening it. Thus a violet's scent seems evanescent. Shakespeare speaks of it as 'the perfume and the suppliance of a minute'.) The botanist John Parkinson regarded the violet as his 'choise flower of delight'; Goethe was reputed to wander around Weimar sowing violet seeds from a supply in his pocket. But violet fancying really took off with Napoleon, and even more with the advent of the Parma.

A bit of botany first. The genus *Viola* is a fairly large one, incorporating some 500 pansies, violas and violets. Some are scented, but the really powerfully perfumed wild specimens are mainly violets, in particular the appropriately named *V. odorata*. Though most of history, until deliberate crossbreeding began, *V. odorata* was the principal fragrant violet. Single, violet-coloured (sometimes white), it is native to Britain and much of Europe.

Napoleon was famously fond of violets, or so the propaganda had it, and *V. odorata* or one of its numerous sports must have been the object of his affection. His first wife Josephine grew violets in the gardens of Malmaison, and they at length became the Napoleonic symbol; Bonaparte vowed to return from his exile in Elba 'when the violets bloom'. (He did so, but there turned out to be no violets at Waterloo.) With the restoration of the monarchy, Napoleon's old officers wore violets in their buttonholes as a sign of loyalty. By the time Napoleon III took the throne and Empress Eugénie the lead in fashion, the lowly violet was well on its way to true iconic status.

This might not necessarily have happened, however, had it not been for the activities of plant breeders, and those obscure but ingenious collectors who tracked down and introduced into cultivation the particularly intensely scented variety that came to be known as the Parma violet. Until well into the nineteenth century, most new forms had arisen spontaneously through accidental mutations. Now that there was profit to be made, improvements emerged, though the process was halting, slow, and not for the faint-hearted. 'A patient, persevering, and unrewarded race,' was the way E.J. Perfect, a writer on violet history, described the men who came up with such important cultivars as 'La Violette des Quatre Saisons', with its long blooming period, and many more.

The problem for the breeders was less a shortage of plausible candidates for crossing than the way that certain violets set seed – or fail to. In nature, members of the viola family are absolutely promiscuous, producing sub-species with almost indecent abandon. (In his splendid *Flora Britannica* Richard Mabey notes how fifty years ago botanists cataloguing British violets practically lost their way, naming no less than eighteen different types of hairy violet (*V. hirta*) alone. The number has now been radically reduced.) When it comes to making deliberate crosses, however, breeders are inhibited by the fact that many violets – *V. odorata* among them – are cleistogamous. Their visible blossoms play no part in reproduction; seed is produced inside closed (and hidden) later blossoms without any need for external fertilization, because the plant is self-pollinating. (The seeds, incidentally, contain a substance attractive to ants, which drag them away and sow them willy-nilly.) In the case of Parma violets, the problem is even worse: they almost never set seed at all, reproducing instead by runners.

The true origin of Parmas is a mystery. Tender, double, the most spectacular and fragrant violet of all, they are also the most demanding to grow. Once assumed to be a variety of *V. odorata* – logically enough, given their powerful scent – this derivation has been challenged recently; Parmas might possibly comprise a distinct species. In any case, they have always been precious. They probably came with Venetian or Genoese traders from Asia Minor or the Near East to Italy or Portugal, and in the eighteenth century to other parts of Europe. Their name changed as they moved around, being variously called 'Portuguese' or 'Neapolitan' or (in France) 'La Violette de Parme'. 'Parma' finally stuck, in part because of the horticultural activities of Napoleon's second wife, the violet-loving Austrian princess Marie Louise, who raised the eponymous plants in Parma itself. Two cultivars now bear her name, the deep violet-mauve 'Marie Louise' and the lavender-mauve 'Duchesse de Parme'.

Though he does not seem to have called them by that name, it appears likely that the violets grown in Sir Joseph Banks's garden at Isleworth near London between 1816 and 1819 were Parmas. Banks's gardener was a skilled plantsman called Isaac Oldaker, previously employed by the Tsar of Russia at the Imperial Gardens at Ropsha, who wrote a detailed report of his success with the violets in the *Transactions* of the Horticultural Society. (Oldaker was incidentally talented in other ways. Having been retired by the Tsar on a temporary disability pension for his asthma in 1812, he managed – with the help of doctors' notes – to go on getting the money every year for the next forty years. Try that on your Human Resources department.)

To begin with, violet growers concentrated near big cities, gradually moving out to remoter areas as air pollution affected production. Urban centres remained the big markets, however – everyone from the grandest ladies to city clerks seemed to need a bouquet or a buttonhole. In 1845, the French novelist and garden writer Alphonse Karr remarked: 'Go to the opera and you will see 200 women with bunches of violets in their hands.' The most refined customers were catered to: one of the French breeder Armand Millet's most successful introductions, 'Madame Millet,' was praised in 1884 as being 'an exact match for the fashion shade of heliotrope'. A violet buttonhole seems to have been *de rigeur* for intrepid horsewomen out hunting foxes. But the favourite format for balls and weddings and soirées was the flattened bouquet or *monté plat*, sometimes made up with snowdrops or perhaps with violets surrounding a white camellia.

One way and another, usually by fortuitous discovery in a bed full of more normal varieties, a range of new cultivars emerged onto the market. The resoundingly named Count Savorgnin di Brazza, raising violets near Udine, originated the pure white Parma henceforth called 'Conte di Brazza' (although it picked up another name when an English grower christened it 'Swanley White', thus causing decades of confusion). Millet, working in Bourg-le-Reine near Paris, produced a number of differently coloured scented single violets, then went on to grow several new Parmas. Certain cultivars were easier to grow than others, some hardier or more floriferous or more readily acclimatized to conditions in different countries. Most, however, suffered eventually from disease and pests such as nematodes in the greenhouses where they had to be grown, or from weakness brought on through repeated reproduction by runners or division rather than seed. Stems became less sturdy and plants more susceptible to cold weather. Rumours spread that blossoms were becoming less fragrant, though this was probably a canard stemming from the introduction of weakly scented American varieties.

And then there were more subtle problems. In his classic survey *Violets*, Roy Coombs describes how the replacement of gaslight or oil lamps by electric lights in the early twentieth century made the hitherto-popular darker coloured Parmas appear to be almost black; they fell out of fashion in favour of lighter sorts.

The years before World War I were the last really good ones for scented violets. From California (between 1901 and 1912 nearly fifty nurseries were growing violets in San Mateo County) to Italy to Germany, demand was strong, with many new cultivars. Improved varieties of single violets (as opposed to the more pernickety tender double Parmas) did especially well. But wartime fuel shortages – plus, of course, changing fashion – dramatically reduced the number of nurseries. The business had always been hideously labour-intensive (modern growers figure it can take two and a half hours to pick a box of blooms worth £15 wholesale); commercial production of any violets, even field-grown varieties, is impossible to mechanize. And now labour was short.

Except in the south of France, where perfume makers continued to buy violets until chemical scents got the upper hand, the war virtually wiped out French production. A few nurseries lingered on the Hudson, and more in Cornwall, Devon and Dorset supplying both the cut-flower trade and the manufacturers of soap and toiletries. Well into the 1920s and 1930s you could buy sweet violets by the bunch in London. It isn't easy today. In fact, a request for violets is more likely than not to be answered with a pot of African violets (which are no relation, scentless, and have been around only since 1892). In the 1960s the former Rosewarne Experimental Horticultural Station in Cornwall gave up trialling violets altogether.

As Roy Coombs makes plain, it is no longer a question of survival for the violet industry, but of survival for the cultivars themselves. A number of the once-famous Parmas are extinct, while the ones that remain do so thanks only to devoted gardeners and a few nurseries selling them in pots. (He suggests, incidentally, that anyone hankering to grow Parmas try 'Duchesse de Parme' first; it is usually the easiest.)

Odd events a few years ago suggest that all may not be lost for lost cultivars. Violet fanciers looking over the site of a nursery in Winchester that had been closed down for a dozen years were surprised to come upon flourishing examples of some rare varieties that had survived neglect to grow wild. Still more startling was the discovery in 1986, after no less than fifty years of abandonment, of violets bred at Clevedon, Somerset, by a brilliant market gardener named George Lee. Thought to be extinct, they were found growing, quite insouciantly, in the back gardens of the subdivision that had been built over Lee's fields and greenhouses after World War II. Lee no doubt would have been gratified, if only as a man who knew the value of a bit of publicity when he could get it. After all, he was the one who developed an exquisite, finely scented violet-purple sweet violet, named it 'Victoria Regina', and made a point of sending a large bunch to Queen Victoria at Balmoral every year.

A Little History

In 1891, the redoubtable Canon Henry Ellacombe estimated that up to that time no less than 100,000 books had been written on the subject of gardening. This didn't stop the Canon from writing several more, nor has it (fortunately) deterred the historian and biographer Jenny Uglow. Much of the charm of her breakneck canter* through the entire history of British gardening arises from the fact that nothing about her subject appears to strike her as boring or over-familiar. She simply wades in, happily retailing anecdotes, odd facts, pocket portraits and occasional large generalities. The result may not be original, but it is a delight.

And how not? Garden history is full of wonderful stuff, and British garden history more than most. What about Sir William Chambers and his 'horrid' garden, based on a large misconception of Chinese practice, in which 'sudden explosions, electric shocks and fearful sounds' combined with distant views of gibbets to give the visitor a frisson? ('The "horrid" garden was altogether too alarming for an astonished public,' Uglow observes.) Or Sir Walter Raleigh's eccentric half-brother Adrian Gilbert, a mystically inclined horticulturist who called himself 'a true Adamist' and produced a garden described by one bemused

---

* *A Little History of British Gardening* by Jenny Uglow (London 2004).

visitor as 'such a deal of intricate setting, grafting, planting, inoculating, railing, hedging, plashing, turning, winding, and returning circular, triangular, quadrangular, orbicular, oval, and every way curiously and chargeably conceited.' Gilbert's near contemporary Sir Henry Wotton might well have approved; *his* ideal garden was 'a delightful confusion,' and in the eighteenth century writer Batty Langley fumed 'Is there anything more shocking than a *stiff regular garden?*'

As Uglow makes plain, the British love of gardening (confused or otherwise) goes back very far indeed, although it is sometimes difficult to distinguish horticulture from farming or simply growing food to eat. Pleasure gardening demanded the sort of sophistication and wealth possessed by the Roman invaders or the later monasteries. The spirit was always there: a tenth-century Anglo-Saxon translated the term garden as a *luffendliche stede* – literally 'a lovely place'. But in most respects real gardening history, in the sense of design and plantsmanship, emerged only the with the Tudors in the fifteenth century. At this point, and for a long time afterwards, it was a business for royalty and the gentry – for those, in short, with plenty of labour at their disposal. Land, too: Sir Francis Bacon (see page 138) figured that no garden of less than 30 acres should be considered.

Much of *A Little History* is therefore concerned with great gardens – the royal demesnes like Hampton Court, the vast classical constructions like Stourhead and Stowe, the grand country estates pictured by Kip or transformed by 'Capability' Brown. They were, after all, the places where new fashions in plants, landscaping and design first showed themselves. They also tended to provide subject matter for writers and artists. Even in the nineteenth century, by which time horticulture was a matter of far wider interest and men like John Claudius Loudon were busily turning out books and magazines for an eager middle class audience, it was the rich who still made most of the running with their glasshouses, pineta, parks and gardeners in green baize aprons. To build a rock garden in the form of a scaled-down version of the Matterhorn, complete with cast-iron chamois, you needed the disposable income of a Sir Frank Crisp.

I'm pleased to say that before Jenny Uglow finishes her story, she brings us round to what gardening has become for most of us. With a few exceptions, it's not so grand. Professional gardeners are pretty thin on the ground these days. Some of the slack has been taken up by machines, so instead of the placid click of secateurs in the great rose alleys there is likely to be the clatter of a hedge-clipper, or the whine of the strimmer. Fashion still displays its force, the *Verbena bonariensis* giving way to the wildflower meadow, the exotic grasses to the agapanthus. But orthodoxy is dead, if it ever existed. Meanwhile, television programmes, garden centres supplying a range of plants unimaginable a generation ago, and a vast and well-organized garden-visiting system centered on *The Yellow Book* are all doing much to shape the kind of gardens we are making in what she calls 'the brilliant, difficult, fruitful mixed world of today'. Whether this an improvement or not is a moot point. In any case, there is a lot to be said for looking back at the way it was.

The Wandering Plants
of Meriwether Lewis

Americans have a way of getting extremely worked up about their own history (I should know, I'm an American) and a perfect recent example is the amount of publicity – books, articles, television programmes, an infinity of websites – generated by the 200th anniversary of the Lewis and Clark Expedition. For those who may somehow have failed to hear about it, this was the two-year-long transcontinental journey launched by President Thomas Jefferson in the spring of 1804. Its purpose was find a route to the Pacific Coast across the largely unexplored plains, mountains and deserts west of the Mississippi, and at the same time to collect scientific, geographic and cultural information about everything to be found there from grizzly bears to Mandan raincoats. And plants. Jefferson, an enthusiastic gardener, was especially interested in plants.

It's not hard to see why the expedition has so caught the national imagination. Much of the landscape along its route has hardly changed in 200 years, especially in the inhospitable reaches of mountains and forest and vast barren flats that begin where the Rockies rear up out of the Great Plains. Of course the buffalo are gone, and the Indians – now properly called Native Americans – have long since been driven into reservations or decimated by disease. But the least sensitive tourist, motoring up the broad

Green River valley beneath the louring snow-capped peaks of the Wind River Range, or strolling through a lodgepole pine wilderness on the Gros Ventre, or peering into a preciptous gorge along the Snake River, is likely to feel a twinge of historical sympathy for Meriwether Lewis and William Clark, and the Mountain Men – rough-cut fur trappers – who wandered the region before and after them. I know I have. That country touches you deeply.

Still, the romance ought not to obscure the fact that the Corps of Discovery was above all a scientific expedition, as hard-headed and technical in purpose as an Explorer launch from Cape Canaveral. Jefferson certainly looked at it that way; from the outset he made certain that Lewis particularly – a former army officer who had become his secretary – was equipped to perform the necessary intellectual duties. He dispatched him to Philadelphia, then the cultural capital of the young United States, to receive training in astronomy, anatomy and medicine from such renowned figures as Andrew Ellicot, Caspar Wister and Benjamin Rush. And from Benjamin Smith Barton, professor at the University of Pennsylvania and the nation's premier botanist (and author of the first American botanical textbook), he was to learn taxonomy, as well as how to collect and dry specimens. Barton was an old friend of Jefferson's. The President intended to have him study and assist in the publication of the plants that Lewis collected.

Lewis learned his lessons well; the notes he made during the journey show exceptional competence, apart from his ingenious but rarely conventional spelling (e.g. pittatoe, convolvalist, applycation, piennial). So far as plants are concerned, it has been calculated that he collected no fewer than 202 different varieties, including 176 previously unknown species. There almost certainly would have been more – disasters such as boats overturning, buried caches rotting, and specimens burned in accidental fires unquestionably reduced the number that reached civilization again. Nor was their arrival on the East Coast the end of the story. In fact, the post-expedition saga of Lewis's plants is in some ways as colourful as the great overland trek itself, involving as it does several extraordinary characters, subterfuge and skulduggery, and a few still unsolved mysteries.

In all, two batches of plant material – dried herbarium specimens, seeds, and even a few live plants – reached Jefferson from Lewis. The first lot, consisting mostly of plants found along the Mississippi and the Missouri River as far north as the Mandan village where the expedition spent the winter of 1804–5, arrived in August 1805; the second, a smaller group containing cuttings and more seeds, as well as more dried specimens, was delivered by Lewis personally when the Corps returned in 1807. A major loss was the collection made further up the Missouri in the spring of 1805, on the way west. It had been cached in the foothills of the Rockies but was destroyed in the disastrous spring floods of 1806 before it could be retrieved.

Jefferson, who famously commented that 'the greatest service that can be rendered to any country is to add a useful plant to its culture', must have been delighted to get Lewis's haul. The herbarium specimens he forwarded to Barton, whom he hoped would get on with the work of classifying them; the seeds he planted in his own garden or sent for propagation to the best plantsmen he knew. These included Bernard M'Mahon, Philadelphia seed merchant and horticulturist par excellence, and William Hamilton, wealthy owner of a splendid estate called Woodlands outside Philadelphia. Hamilton's challenge was to grow a kind of tobacco (*Nicotiana quadrivalvis*) used by the Mandans and the Arikawas, although Jefferson had a low opinion of tobacco generally, believing its culture was 'productive of infinite wretchedness'. For his part, M'Mahon managed to cultivate some two dozen species all told, including seven currants (*Ribes aureum* and *R. odoratum* among them) and snowberry (*Symphoricarpus albus*), and did so well with the newly discovered Oregon grape holly (*Mahonia aquifolium*) that it now bears his name. Jefferson himself grew beans, corn and – less successfully – a kind of wild salsify. A so-called 'flowering pea' flourished for him at Monticello, but today nobody knows exactly what it was.

A particular find, brought east by Lewis from a St Louis garden and raised by both M'Mahon and Hamilton, would become enormously popular. The Osage orange (*Maclura pomifera*) was by the middle of the nineteenth century the most widely planted shrub in America. Its thorns and willingness to be sheared made it ideal hedging material. According to Peter Hatch, director of the Monticello Gardens, some 60,000 miles of Osage orange hedging was planted in 1868 alone. Only the invention of barbed wire brought its reign to a close.

It was Lewis and Clark's dried specimens, however, that caused the most difficulty and, ultimately, controversy. Although it was a time when hundreds of hitherto unknown plants were being found, described and named, there was still intense competition to publish first, and thus receive credit for the discovery. Priority was precious. Predictably, this situation gave rise to a certain amount of unacademic behaviour.

Contrary to Jefferson's expectations, Professor Barton, having received Lewis's scrupulously prepared, mounted and catalogued specimens, had still done nothing at all with them by the time the expedition returned in 1806. Barton claimed ill-health; botanical historian James Reveal suggests that the professor had a feckless streak, and when called upon to produce he rarely came through. In any event, when M'Mahon proposed a solution to the frustrated Lewis, then under intense pressure to prepare his notes, journals and other material for publication as soon as possible, he apparently leaped at it. Living at M'Mahon's house in Philadelphia was a German in his early thirties named Frederick Pursh. A moderately experienced botanist, plant collector and gardener, Pursh would be able to examine the specimens and formally describe them on Lewis's behalf.

Pursh remains a somewhat shadowy figure, evidently sour and not much loved, with 'tartaresque features and . . . rough-hewn behaviour' in the words of one contemporary. Since coming from Europe in 1799 he had worked at several noted gardens in the Philadelphia area, including Hamilton's Woodlands, and was acquainted with such prominent local plantsmen as William Bartram and Henry Muhlenberg. After an angry break with Hamilton (who, according to M'Mahon, 'had not used him well'), he was taken up as a collector by Barton, who harboured large and fanciful ideas of writing a new flora of North America. For two years Pursh had been travelling the backwoods of Virginia and Pennsylvania hunting for plants for Barton. He must have learned about the first batch of material Lewis sent when it first reached Philadelphia. Meeting Lewis in May, 1806, he seems to have agreed readily to describe and draw the plants, along with the remainder that the explorer brought with him, 'for the purpose of inserting them in the account of his *Travels* which [Lewis] was then engaged in preparing for the press'. Lewis paid Pursh a seventy-dollar advance and turned over to him his entire collection of herbarium specimens. It was a major commitment, and, as it turned out, not the wisest one.

By 1807, Pursh had completed work on the plants, except for a few where he needed to check details with Lewis. Lewis, unfortunately, was not available. Upon his return from the West, he had collected his rewards for the successful expedition – back pay at double rate, a warrant for 1,600 acres of land, and appointment as Governor of Upper Louisiana – and made a few ineffectual gestures toward arranging a publishing contract for his and Clark's journals. He also began drinking. A couple of marriage attempts fell through. His close relationship with Jefferson cooled, partly because of his drinking and partly because of his delay in taking up his gubernatorial duties in St Louis, which he finally reached in 1808. The job was a fiasco, quite beyond Lewis's administrative capabilities. *En route* back to Washington in October 1809, in a country tavern in Tennessee, he shot himself in the head.

Meanwhile, Pursh found himself in limbo. He had not been paid, but he had the plants, he had the drawings and the descriptions. They were, to say the least, exciting: he later remarked that of the 155 specimens he examined, 'not above a dozen plants [were] known to me to be natives of North America – the rest being either entirely new or little known, and among them at least six distinct and new genera'. The temptation to publish them must have been great, but he had no right to do so. In need of income and despairing of Lewis's return, in April 1809 he went to New York to work in the Elgin Botanic Garden Dr David Hosack was building on the site of what is now Rockefeller Center. With him he took his descriptions, most of his drawings and – quite without permission – roughly a quarter of the original herbarium specimens from the Lewis and Clark collection.

The question of who would get credit for discovering the new species was still more pressing after word came of Lewis's death. M'Mahon wrote to Jefferson lamenting the news and expressing his concern that any of the '*new* living plants' he had raised 'should make their way into the hands of any Botanist, either in America or Europe, who might rob Mr Lewis of the right he had to first describe and name his own discoveries'. Indeed, he went on, 'I had strong reason to believe that this opportunity was coveted by _____, which made me still more careful of the plants.' What name did M'Mahon delicately omit? It might well have been Pursh, whose ambitions must have been familiar to him. How much more directly might he have phrased it he had known of Pursh's theft; in the same letter M'Mahon claims still to be safely guarding the whole collection of dried plants.

In 1810, Lewis's fellow explorer William Clark arrived in Philadelphia to pick up the pieces. He took back the balance of the specimens held by M'Mahon and apparently forwarded payment to Pursh for the work he had done, although there is no evidence that Clark actually got Pursh's drawings. The retrieved herbarium material went to the American Philosophical Society, and may have been passed back to Dr Barton in the doubtlessly vain hope that he would work on it. Somewhere along the way, thirty more specimens vanished and have never been found.

Pursh bided his time, working in New York and collecting in the Caribbean for the Elgin Garden. Finally, in late 1811, having in customary fashion fallen out with Hosack, he sailed off to London, bearing a large number of specimens, not only the Lewis and Clark lot but examples of many of the plants he had collected for Hosack and Barton. He was now determined to press ahead with publication, ethically or otherwise.

London was an ideal place to work. Several large private libraries and collections were available to him, as well as the resources of the famed Linnean Society, and he found a patron in a rich botanical amateur named Aylmer Bourke Lambert. At first, he ventured modest journal publication, placing an account in the *Botanical Magazine* of the gumbo lily (now *Mentzelia decapetala*), which he named *Bartonia decapetala* after his old master. But he soon had devised a far more ambitious plan, a plan that would bring him into more controversy and, it must be said, more double-dealing before he could accomplish it. Pursh determined to publish a comprehensive North American flora. What with the plants and drawings he had brought with him from America, he was well on his way to his goal.

But he could not help but be aware that haste was necessary. The botanical riches of the American continent were readily available to any plant hunter with the energy and nerve to find them. And it so happened that at least one such man was already in the field. When Pursh left Philadephia for New York, he had been succeeded in Professor Barton's employ by a young Englishman named Thomas Nuttall. A slightly whimsical personality, Nuttall was a clear genius as a plant collector and a bit of a joke otherwise. Barton himself, in a letter of introduction, described him as 'a young man distinguished by innocence of character'. For all his 'innocence', however, Nuttall was prepared to brave the worst challenges of weather, terrain and unfriendly natives to collect an extraordinary range of new botanical species, including many that Lewis and Clark had found, on the Upper Missouri and the Great Plains, as well as further east. In 1811, loaded with duplicates of his seeds, bulbs and dried specimens (a set went to Barton, of course), Nuttall sailed back to England with publication very much in mind. His travelling companion, an older botanist named John Bradbury, was caught by the outbreak of the War of 1812 and forced to stay in America, having already shipped his own collections to England.

Pursh met Nuttall in London in the spring of 1812. Even then, Nuttall's seeds were germinating at a nursery in Chelsea and his own book, a *Catalogue of New and Interesting Plants Collected in Upper Louisiana and Principally on the River Missouri, North America*, must have been well advanced, because it was published in the autumn of 1813. But – apparently according to the agreement Nuttall had made with the owners of the nursery, who published the book – his name appears nowhere on it. Thus he beat Pursh to the wire – but received none of the credit for priority.

Frederick Pursh, left to his dubious devices, plodded ahead in what was now a fairly clear field. The inbred nature of Britain's botanical community meant that he had had access, via his patron Lambert, to virtually all of the collections of American plants in the country – not excluding Nuttall's and, before long, that of Nuttall's fellow collector Bradbury, who had put together an exceptional group of hitherto unknown species. Pursh's *Flora Americae septentrionalis* ('Flora of North America') emerged in two volumes at the end of 1813. The main text covered, among other species, 132 of the plants brought back by the Lewis and Clark expedition, while a last-minute supplement was devoted to forty plants collected by Bradbury. In his own crafty way, Pursh had in the end triumphed.

To see what this meant, you have only to browse through a handbook like Mark Griffiths' *Index of Garden Plants*. Vine maple (*Acer circinatum*), evergreen huckleberry (*Vaccinium ovatum*), Lewis's monkey flower (*Mimulus lewisii*), ocean spray (*Holodiscus discolor*), shrubby penstemon (*Penstemon fructicosus*), Oregon maple (*Acer macrophyllum*) – all were collected by Lewis; all bear Pursh's name as 'author'. Even the so-called prairie potato or Indian breadroot that the Corps of Discovery made so much of – and would probably have starved without – is listed as *Psorlea esculenta* Pursh. The same treatment was accorded species first collected by Nuttall and Bradbury.

Nuttall was furious. 'It was surely not honourable,' he wrote, 'to snatch from me the little imaginary credit due my enthusiastic researches made at the most imminent risk of personal safety.' Bradbury was no happier. In the preface to a later account of his travels, he explained that he had intended to describe his own findings, but 'my design was frustrated, by my collection having been submitted to the inspection of a person by the name of Pursh'.

On Pursh's behalf, it should be noted that his efforts probably saved a great deal of historically important information and material from oblivion. He gave generous credit to Lewis and Clark for what they had achieved and named plants after them (*Lewisia* and *Clarkia*, neither, it has to be said, spectacular). Nor did he benefit much from winning the publication race. His subsequent career, apparently hampered if not actually dominated by an increasing reliance on liquor, went gradually downhill. A journey to Russia, after which he prepared and published a catalogue of plants in a grand duke's garden, was followed by a commission from Lord Selkirk to be botanist at the Scottish grandee's newly founded Red River settlement in Manitoba. Pursh got no further than Montreal. After a time spent in desultory collecting along the St Lawrence, he lost everything in a house fire. In 1818, alone and destitute, he died.

Nuttall, on the other hand, scarcely broke stride on his way to becoming one of the greatest of all American naturalists. His 1818 book *Genera of North American Plants and a Catalogue of Species* far outshone any previous work – including Pursh's – for comprehensiveness, accuracy and, above all, personal observation and detail. Moreover, it firmly established Nuttall as the first to describe and names hundreds of American species.

Throughout his long life, Nuttall never stopped travelling, looking, making notes on what he saw – plants, birds, animals, whatever fascinating things fell beneath his gaze, a true field worker. In this, perhaps, he had much in common with Meriwether Lewis in the wilds of the yet-to-be discovered West.

Incredibly enough, most of Lewis's herbarium specimens survived their many journeys, to find rest at last in a single collection back in Philadelphia. Nearly all of the plants Pursh took with him to London joined the huge collection of his patron Aylmer Bourke Lambert. At Lambert's death in 1842, the collection – amounting by then to some 50,000 sheets – was auctioned off. A young American named Edward Tuckerman chanced to pick up one lot labelled 'American plants' for a few pounds; it turned out to contain all but nine of Lewis's plants, together with more from Nuttall and others. The missing nine eventually ended in Kew; Tuckerman passed his lucky find on to the Academy of Natural Sciences in Philadelphia. They are still there, having finally been rejoined by the group evidently deposited by Barton or his heirs at the American Philosophical Society; these latter specimens were only rediscovered in the 1890s. Some of the sheets still bear notes in Lewis's spidery handwriting, telling where he found and picked the plants whose faded remains are attached.

INDEX